An Introduction to Computers in Information Science

Second Edition

by

SUSAN ARTANDI

The Scarecrow Press, Inc.
Metuchen, N.J.   1972

Dedicated

TO MY FAMILY

Copyright 1972 by Susan Artandi

Library of Congress Cataloging in Publication Data

Artandi, Susan.
    An introduction to computers in information science.

    Includes bibliographies.
    1. Information storage and retrieval systems.
I. Title.
Z699.A73 1972   029.7   72-1136
ISBN 0-8108-0485-9

PREFACE

The second edition of this book represents an extensive revision of the first edition, published in 1968, to incorporate new developments in this rapidly changing field.

The overall scope and objectives of the book, however, remain the same. It is an introduction to the field of information science and technology, with particular emphasis on document organization. Its point of view is general in the sense that it attempts to deal with types of problems rather than particular systems. When particular systems are described they are used as examples rather than as models.

The method of presentation is expository at the introductory level. While differing points of view are frequently noted, the book is not intended to provide definitive critical evaluation. Relevant research is reviewed to indicate current thinking and activities in the field.

Part I gives an overview of the field of information science and technology. Part II, on the theoretical aspects of document retrieval, emphasizes the intellectual problems that apply to document organization at all levels.

Part III includes a rudimentary explanation of the basic characteristics of the equipment involved in applications of computers to information science and a discussion of representative machine applications. The latter is organized by type of application, with examples for each type. The flow charts which accompany the descriptions of applications were kept general to provide the reader with a simplified overview of the various methods.

The references at the end of each chapter have been updated since the first edition. However, since these references have been chosen with the needs of the teacher in mind--particularly the teacher of this subject at the introductory level--a number of older, standard references continue to be cited.

It is hoped that by introducing the reader to some of the problems and activities of information science and technology the book will stimulate interest in the study of the field at a more advanced level.

Susan Artandi

Princeton, N. J.
September 1971

CONTENTS

PART I: INFORMATION SCIENCE AND TECHNOLOGY

CHAPTER 1. INTRODUCTION

The Discipline   15

The Literature of Information Science and
    Technology   19

Educational Programs   20

Quo Vadis?   21

PART II: THEORETICAL ASPECTS OF
DOCUMENT ORGANIZATION

CHAPTER 2. GENERALIZED VIEW OF DOCUMENT
            RETRIEVAL

Document Retrieval Versus Data Retrieval   26

Document Description and Representation   27

Elements of Retrieval Systems   29

CHAPTER 3. PROCESSING OF DOCUMENTS FOR
            INPUT

Subject Indexing   35

Word Indexing   37

Index Languages   39

Lists of Terms   42

Pre-Coordination and Post-Coordination   44

The Concept of Sets	48
Subsets	49
Combination of Sets	50
Index Language Devices	53
Consistency of Indexing	56
Citation Indexing	57

CHAPTER 4. THE RETRIEVAL OF DOCUMENTS

The File of Document Representations	63
File Structures	65
File Processes	67
Searching	67
Query Formulation	69
Feedback	71
System Characteristics and Search Strategies	72
Evaluation of Retrieval Systems	74
Evaluative Measures	75
Relevance Experimentation	77
The Cranfield Experiments	78
The MEDLARS Evaluation Study	80
Cost-Effectiveness of Retrieval Systems	81

PART III: COMPUTER BASED SYSTEMS

CHAPTER 5. COMPUTER HARDWARE AND SOFTWARE

The Digital Computer	87
The Binary Concept	90
Binary Representation of Decimal Numbers	92
Data Representation for Computer Processing	93
Data Representation for Input	94
Keyboarding	94
Punched Cards	95

Paper Tape	95
Magnetic Tape	97
Optical Character Recognition	102
Voice Recognition	104
Graphic Input	105

Output Representation 106

Printers	106
Computer Composition	109
Microfilm Output	110
Voice Output	111

Storage	112
Storage Devices	113
Core Storage	114
Disk Storage	115
Magnetic Drum Storage	118
Data Cells	119

Programming Languages 119

Computer Time-Sharing 123

Definition of Time-Sharing	124
Kinds of Time-Sharing	125
Terminals	127
Human Factors in Time-Sharing	129

CHAPTER 6. REPRESENTATIVE MACHINE APPLICATIONS

Introduction 133

Mechanical Retrieval of Manually Organized Information Combined with the Production of a File for Manual Searching 134

Examples:

MEDLARS System	135
Indexing	136
Input Subsystem	138
Retrieval Subsystem	140
Publication Subsystem	140
On-Line Retrieval	143
Performance of the System	143

MARC System 145

    The MARC II Record Format for Monographs 146

Production of a File for Manual Searching from Mechanically Organized Information 151

    Example:

    KWIC Index 151

Mechanical Matching of Manually Created Interest Profiles with Manually Created Document Surrogates 160

    Example:

    Selective Dissemination of Information (SDI) 160

        User Profiles 161
        Matching Strategies 163
        Overall System Effectiveness 165
        Multiple Data Bases 165

On-Line Retrieval of Manually Organized Information 168

    Examples:

    Project Intrex 168

        The Augmented Catalog Program 169
        Searching the Data Base 170
        Command Language 171
        Text-Access Program 171

    MAC Technical Information Project 172

Production of Printed Indexes 175

Automatic Indexing 177

Machine Translation 180

    Experimental Methods of Machine Translation 182
    Machine-Aided Translation 183

INDEX 185

LIST OF ILLUSTRATIONS

Page

Figure

1. Document Retrieval System--General Model   30
2. Descriptive Tags   36
3. "Tree of Knowledge" Structure   45
4. Venn Diagrams   52
5. Term/Document Matrix   65
6. Information in Analog and Digital Form   88
7. The Organization of the Digital Computer   90
8. Place Value of Binary Numbers   92
9. Decimal Numbers and Their Corresponding Binary Representations   92
10. Keyboarding Methods   94
11. IBM Punched Card   96
12. Paper Tape, Eight-Channel Code   97
13. Magnetic Tape, Seven-Track, Seven-Bit Alphanumeric Code   100
14. Reading Times for Effective Character Rates for Magnetic Tape Records   101
15. Arrangement of Records on Magnetic Tape   102
16. Print Wheel   106
17. Print Chain   107

18.	Wire Printing Dot Patterns	108
19.	5 x 7 Dot Pattern	108
20.	Storage Devices	114
21.	Selecting a Core	115
22.	Character Location	115
23.	Schematic, 163,840 Position Storage	116
24.	Information Arrangement on Disk	117
25.	Head Arrangement, Disk Storage	117
26.	Schematic of Drum Storage	118
27.	Steps Involved in the Translation of the Source Program into the Object Program	122
28.	Block Diagram of the Computer as a Multi-programmed Multiprocessing Time-Shared System	126
29.	Video Terminal	128
30.	Mechanical Retrieval of Manually Organized Information Combined with the Production of a File for Manual Searching--General Diagram	134
31.	MEDLARS--Indexing Worksheet	137
32.	MEDLARS--Input Subsystem	139
33.	MEDLARS--Retrieval Subsystem	141
34.	MEDLARS--Publication Subsystem	142
35.	The MARC System	147
36.	Sample Library of Congress Card in the MARC II Format	148
36a.	Library of Congress Card	149

37. Production of a File for Manual Searching from
Mechanically Organized Information   151

38. Typical Page from a KWIC Index   153

39. KWIC Index Lines and Corresponding Document 154

40. KWIC Bibliography Page   156

41. Steps Involved in the Preparation of the Complete
KWIC Index   157

42. Mechanical Matching of Manually Created Interest
Profiles with Manually Created Document
Surrogates--General Diagram   160

43. Notification Card, Printed Front and Back   163

44. On-Line Retrieval of Manually Organized
Information--General Diagram   168

45. Organization of the MAC Technical Information
Project   173

PART I

INFORMATION SCIENCE
AND TECHNOLOGY

CHAPTER 1

INTRODUCTION

The Discipline

The Literature of Information Science and Technology

Educational Programs

Quo Vadis?

THE DISCIPLINE

There is no generally accepted definition of information science as a distinct discipline. While there have been attempts to define documentation, a term which has become largely synonymous with information science and technology, none of the definitions have been accepted generally. Documentation has been called "librarianship in high gear" and "the group of techniques necessary for the ordered presentation, organization, and communication of recorded (specialized) knowledge in order to give maximum accessibility and utility to the information contained."[1] Other definitions come from the 1961 and 1962 conferences at the Georgia Institute of Technology and the 1965 ADI Symposium on Education for Information Science.

The Georgia Tech conferences provided the following definition of information science:

> The science that investigates the properties and behavior of information, the forces governing the flow of information, and the means of processing information for optimum accessibility and usability. The processes include the origination, dissemination, collection, organization, storage, retrieval, interpretation, and use of information. The field

15

is derived from or related to mathematics, logic, linguistics, psychology, computer technology, operations research, the graphic arts, communications, library science, management, and some other fields.[2]

Although no formal definition of the field resulted from the ADI Symposium on Education for Information Science, a general consensus was reached in the following statement:

> Information science is particularly concerned with stored or recorded messages, their creation as distinguishable marks or documents, their propagation and use. The discipline has two characteristics of science: a pure science component which inquires into the subject without regard to its application, and the applied science component which develops into services and products.[3]

In his introduction to the first volume of the Annual Review of Information Science and Technology, Carlos Cuadra makes the very appropriate observation that "the element that provides whatever degree of cohesiveness now exists in the field, is a shared deep concern with information--its generation, transformation, communication, storage, retrieval and use."[4]

These and other definitions and observations are somewhat less than adequate because they are too broad, or too narrow, or because they fail to distinguish between information science and librarianship. There is no agreement about the nature and scope of information science and technology. What does it consist of? What are its boundaries? What is its relationship to librarianship?[5,6]

This lack of certainty in delimiting the field or in ability to outline its content precisely was especially evident at the 1965 Conference on Education for Information Science held under the sponsorship of the American Documentation Institute. Perhaps one of the more important findings of the Conference was the realization that we need to know better what we mean by information science before we can talk in a meaningful way about educational programs in the field. It was also evident that the relationship between librarianship and information science needs to be clarified to help us to determine the implications of certain core library subjects for information science curricula.

Perhaps one of the reasons that it is so difficult to define the field is that information science frequently deals with things that are qualitatively not too different from contemporary librarianship and that represent the continuation of a single line of development. In other words, in information science we are often concerned with problems that are qualitatively the same as library problems at the same level, except that we are considering them with more sophistication in order to cope with and utilize changes which have occurred in the environment in which we now need to operate.

Other areas of information science try to probe deeper, to discover knowledge that will help to understand better the behavior of information systems. It seeks to find answers to such questions as: What is information and what is its relationship to knowledge? How is information transferred? What is the value of information and what are some of the behavioral patterns that relate to the use of information? How much information can be processed and tolerated by an individual?[7]

Research findings relating to these and similar questions can contribute significantly to the design and operation of information systems.

Today's more extensive and more specialized information needs require more sophisticated approaches to information problems. There is an ever increasing number of people, doing more research and more sophisticated research, who are producing more research results for publication. This, in turn, requires more information from the literature, to enable these people to do more research and to produce more information, and so on, ad infinitum. We must cope with more extensive, intensive and specialized information needs, with new packages of information, and with the tremendous emphasis on up-to-dateness in many fields.

Government reports and preprints are examples of the new packages of information that must be handled. The great increase in specialization influences not only the pattern of generation of information but also the storage and retrieval of this information. The urgency for up-to-dateness in the rapidly growing knowledge in all fields, and particularly in the sciences, provides a challenge and greatly influences the methods of organization of information.

What are the changes that can be utilized in the effective solution of these new challenges? Recent research provides new insights and a more thorough understanding of information science problems, some of which, such as the broad field of document retrieval, have been with us for a long time.

Hardware is becoming more sophisticated, more available, and less expensive. This is true not only of electronic data processing equipment but of other types of equipment that can be applied at various points in the producer-to-user information cycle. However, figures relating to electronic data processing equipment are the most impressive. Computer costs have been steadily decreasing, making computer processing generally more economical and more competitive with manual methods.

Through the realization of the interdisciplinary nature of the field the findings of other disciplines have been increasingly applied in the solution of information science problems. Such fields as mathematics, communication science, linguistics, psychology, systems analysis, and computer science have great pertinence. Automatic translation is an example of a problem in information science whose solution depends to a large extent on advances in linguistic research.

It should be emphasized that the term information science does not imply mechanization. The application of machines is only one aspect of the field; unfortunately, it is often equated with the field itself. A great deal of important non-computer related research work has been going on. Examples are the study of index languages and their effect on retrieval performance; the development of quantitative measures for the evaluation of retrieval performance; the study of the effect of vocabulary control, weights, roles, and links on index language performance; and the study of problems related to thesaurus construction.

Even machine-based systems require a great deal of non-machine work; the human indexer, abstractor, vocabulary builder, and data preparator are still indispensable elements in the total system.

Introduction

THE LITERATURE OF INFORMATION SCIENCE AND TECHNOLOGY

The literature of information science and technology is scattered, poorly controlled and generally uneven in quality. Because of the interdisciplinary nature of the field, pertinent articles often appear in journals of other fields. Writings on information science and technology often contain confusing and frustrating terminology and jargon.

While journal articles are important, a great deal of significant material appears in technical reports or is distributed among members of the profession in the form of preprints. Proliferation of report literature results from the Federal Government's role as a major supporter of research in the field.

Major journals in the field are Journal of the American Society For Information Science (formerly American Documentation), Journal of Documentation, Journal of Chemical Documentation, Information Storage and Retrieval, Journal of Library Automation, and Information Science Abstracts (formerly Documentation Abstracts). Also important are such library oriented journals as Library Resources and Technical Services and Special Libraries, and such hardware-oriented journals as Datamation and Communications of the ACM. There are general science journals, such as Science and Scientific American, which often carry excellent articles on some aspect of the information problem. Because of the universality of information processes, pertinent material is often published in subject-oriented journals which discuss information problems from the point of view of a particular discipline. Examples are Physics Today and Chemical Engineering News.

Professional organizations of interest to the field show fragmentation similar to that in the journal literature. Some organizations, such as American Society for Information Science (formerly American Documentation Institute), and the Fédération International de Documentation (FID), are devoted exclusively to information science and technology. The Special Libraries Association, the Medical Libraries Association and the American Chemical Society are examples of professionally oriented organizations with interest in information science.

EDUCATIONAL PROGRAMS

Educational programs in information science and technology are handicapped by the lack of a clear-cut idea of the nature of the activities and the kinds of skills for which students are to be educated. In addition to the job of training future information specialists, educational programs related to the field also have a responsibility toward the non-specialist, primarily the library school student and the librarian in need of updating his professional training. There is an increasing awareness that, whether or not librarians are directly involved in problems in the area of information science and technology, they should know enough about these areas to enable them to have intelligent and informed opinions about their applicability to library operations. The generalist, when he is faced with a decision, should know how to obtain and evaluate relevant data in order to reach sound decisions. The time has passed when effective library schools can afford to ignore the theories and techniques which, taken together, constitute the field of information science and technology.[8]

Information scientists may work as researchers developing new techniques of information handling, they may be teachers of information science, or they may apply the theories and techniques of information science in the design of information systems. These activities must be translated into viable curricula for academic programs intended for the training of the information scientist.

One of the key questions related to the content of these programs concerns the relationship of the field of information science and the body of knowledge which has evolved from traditional librarianship. In connection with this, as was previously pointed out, one must determine which of the principles and techniques of librarianship are essential to provide a complete and well-balanced base upon which the information science curriculum can build. Existing academic programs in information science frequently reflect the fact that we are not sure just how traditional librarianship and information science and technology should be related in educational programs, and as a result, some of these programs are out of balance and inadequate.

Existing programs intended to train information science specialists may be divided into two broad groups:

those which exist in library schools and those which are developed outside of library schools. An example of the former is the U. C. L. A. program and examples of the latter are the Lehigh University and Georgia Institute of Technology programs.

Generally speaking the library school is taking the responsibility for the information science education of those who are not specialists. The non-specialist, of course, may be a specialist in another field, or he may be a generalist librarian. The non-specialist may be a future administrator who will be called upon to make decisions about mechanized systems and should be able to communicate and consult with experts, or he may be the user or the manager of systems, at various levels of complexity, in varying capacities. Whichever is the case, his professional education, if it is well balanced, should include a basic understanding of the field of information science and technology.

The professional training of the library practitioner is badly in need of updating in terms of the new developments in information science and technology. Efforts in this direction so far have been scattered and not always satisfactorily coordinated. The two major problems related to the continuing education of librarians are to convince them that it is to their benefit to keep up with new developments and to create the suitable educational environment.

QUO VADIS?

In 1963 Shaw wrote:

> It is doubtful that we can radically improve the technology in this field so long as it must rest as heavily as it does on purely empirical foundation. This means that we should be putting massive efforts into the development of a science upon which a better technology may be built.

What would a critical look of the kind that resulted in the above comment show today? Looking at the field, one can detect considerable maturity in the attitude and over-all approach to the subject of information science and technology. No one seems to be looking for instantaneous and final answers, an inclination that so often characterized the past. Rather, there is increasing willingness to face each new problem, examine it carefully, and then try to solve it step-by-step. There seems to be a healthy trend away from trying to solve problems on a purely empirical basis; instead there is a search for theories and for underlying principles. We are on the way to creating a theoretical foundation for the field.

A valid criticism of information science has been that it tends to overlook past experience, that it does not recognize the similarities between current problems and past experience, and that it insists on drawing illusory boundaries between itself and librarianship.[10] This seems to be changing too. Past methods and experiences are being given serious consideration today, especially those which evolved from the field of librarianship. In addition, the way of looking at both past experience and current problems has improved also. We are now approaching traditional methods, as well as new methods, more scientifically than we did only a few years ago. The general maturing of the field will perhaps also help to alleviate what Robert Fairthorne called "terminological corruption."

The changed attitude toward the significance and usefulness of past experience is reflected in some information science curricula. An equally encouraging counter-trend is that traditional library school courses are generally coming to see the value of discussing their subject matter within the broad context of information science. Subjects with such traditional labels as cataloging, classification, or bibliography are taking their rightful places in the over-all task of making information available, rather than being regarded as isolated activities.

Another promising trend is that we are beginning to put the machine in its proper perspective and to think about it as a means, not an end. The approach in which we "take" the machine and build a system around it has fortunately almost disappeared. Instead, through the sound application of the principles and methods of systems analysis, we study a problem and then study the methods and possibly the machines that can help in its solution. This approach has made us realize that there are a number of fundamental intellectual problems that must be solved before machines can be applied to their full advantage.

References

1. Kent, A. "Documentation." *Library Trends,* October 1961.

2. Conferences on Training Science Information Specialists. October 12-13, 1961 and April 12-13, 1962. *Proceedings.* Atlanta, Georgia Institute of Technology, 1962.

3. Reports by working session groups. In: *Symposium on Education for Information Science. Warrenton, Va. September 7-10, 1965. Proceedings.* Washington, D.C., Spartan Books, 1965.

4. Cuadra, Carlos A. "Introduction to the ADI Annual Review." In: *Annual Review of Information Science and Technology,* Vol. 1. Carlos A. Cuadra, ed., New York, Interscience, 1966. pp. 1-14.

5. Borko, Harold. "Information Science: What Is It?", *American Documentation,* 18:3-5, January 1968.

6. Harmon, Glynn. "Opinion Paper--On the Evolution of Information Science." *Journal of the American Society for Information Science,* 22:235-241, July-August 1971.

7. Miller, George A. *The Psychology of Communication.* Baltimore, Maryland, Penguin Books, 1967.

8. Artandi, Susan. "Keeping Up With Machines," *Library Journal,* 90:4715-4717, November 1, 1965.

9. Shaw, Ralph R. "Information Retrieval," *Science,* 140:606-609, May 10, 1963.

10. Baxendale, Phyllis. "Content Analysis, Specification, and Control." In: *Annual Review of Information Science and Technology.* Op. cit., pp. 71-106.

PART II

THEORETICAL ASPECTS OF
DOCUMENT ORGANIZATION

CHAPTER 2

GENERALIZED VIEW OF DOCUMENT RETRIEVAL

Document Retrieval Versus Data Retrieval

Document Description and Representation

Elements of Retrieval Systems

DOCUMENT RETRIEVAL VERSUS DATA RETRIEVAL

Meaningful discussion of the activity known generally as information retrieval requires explicit differentiation between document retrieval and data retrieval. Information retrieval, in the narrow sense of the term, means the retrieval of data or information from a file, as, for example, the retrieval of such pieces of information as the total number of secondary schools in New Jersey, the melting point of copper, or the name of the user who has a certain book checked out. This type of retrieval assumes the existence of a file which allows direct access to the information itself. Handbooks used in science and technology are conventional examples of such a file, while an inventory figure retrieved from a computer memory implies a machine searchable file. Most systems that are loosely referred to as information retrieval systems are, in fact, document retrieval systems because they do not provide direct access to the information itself. Instead, they are designed to retrieve documents which should, with some degree of certainty, contain the desired information. Using the previous example, this means that in a document retrieval system one will retrieve documents which contain information on the melting point of copper and not the melting point figure itself. In this case the user is at least one step removed from the actual information and must search the retrieved document for the information he is seeking. The file that is searched in this case consists of document descriptions rather than data. Examples of such files are card catalogs, printed indexes, and computer indexes to books and articles.

It should be pointed out, however, that files essentially containing document descriptions frequently may also contain directly retrievable data; as, for example, the birthdate of an author or the name of a publisher on a catalog card. This, however, is not the primary purpose for which these files were constructed.

Management information systems, whose function is to provide management with the information it needs to understand, plan, operate, and control its business, are interesting examples of data retrieval files. While document retrieval systems can be, and frequently are, important elements in management information systems, the primary objective of management information systems is to organize data usually generated within an organization so that it can be retrieved, as needed, for improved decision making. The primary concern of this book, however, is document retrieval since the majority of existing non-numerical retrieval systems are in this category.

DOCUMENT DESCRIPTION AND REPRESENTATION

The discussion which follows is based on a generalized model of document retrieval assuming that a set of functional characteristics exists for information organization systems. While every system may not have all of these characteristics, all systems have some of them, and the systematic discussion of the presence, the absence, and the nature of these characteristics should serve as a useful, orderly, and fairly uniform base for the description of various systems. The approach should also help to determine the function and relative importance of various system characteristics.

Organization of documents for retrieval assumes that it is possible to describe the content and other characteristics of documents by assigning descriptive tags to them, or by representing their content in the form of an abstract or an extract. It is also assumed that the searching of a file of document surrogates that are linked to document references can serve as a satisfactory substitute for the scanning of the entire collection, and that it will indicate the existence and location of or the absence of items relevant to an information request.[1] This process of tagging items to indicate what they are about and where they may be found is called, by Fairthorne,[2] "marking and parking."

Inherent in the concept of document surrogation is a degree of imprecision, the extent of which is largely dependent on the effectiveness with which document description and representation is accomplished.

We organize documents because we want to avoid scanning an entire collection in order to find information, and because we want to make possible the examination of only the relevant part of the collection, the part which will most likely contain the required information. Theoretically, we should be able to find what we want by examining the entire collection, but this becomes impractical once the collection has grown beyond a small number of items. Instead, we reduce the amount of material to be examined by organizing the collection through the "recognition of useful similarities between documents and the establishment of useful groups (sets) based on these similarities."[3]

In other words, the objective of indexing is to describe documents and other records in a succinct manner, assigning their information to a limited number of particular classes. A search of the store is then reduced to the examination of a certain class or a certain number of classes. This limits the search to those documents or records judged to be likely containers of the desired information.

The particular way in which "marking and parking" is achieved will vary according to the retrieval system that is used. The total number of approved subject tags that may be used in marking constitutes the index language of the retrieval system. Whether marks are natural language terms or notation, their function is the same; they are intended to indicate what the document is about.

Once index tags have been substituted for documents and have been accepted to stand for the documents, they become the means of communication with the system. Their number and their relationships to each other will determine the characteristics of this communication; its pattern will vary according to the manner in which index language features are used to achieve the objectives of the search. The effectiveness of the indexing system will, in large measure, be determined by the effectiveness of the classes it establishes in accommodating and screening the information to be organized and the information contained in the search descriptions.

It should be remembered, however, that tags other than those indicating subject content can be important elements in the complete document description.[4] Examples of non-subject tags are those which indicate such document characteristics as language, level of presentation, physical form, etc. There is currently a great deal of experimentation to ascertain the relative usefulness of this type of information in document description. Project Intrex at MIT has compiled an extensive list of potentially useful non-subject tags, which are assigned to materials included in their augmented catalog to test their usefulness.[5] (Project Intrex is described in detail in the section on representative machine applications.) In our discussion, however, we will be concerned primarily with methods intended to describe the subject content of documents. Discussion will be concerned with steps which should facilitate the identification of the right informational materials in response to given information needs within the framework and limitations of the materials that are part of a given system. We shall not deal with certain important aspects of the total information cycle, such as selection/or acquisition of materials for input to the system or the dissemination of materials at the output end.

ELMENTS OF RETRIEVAL SYSTEMS

Document retrieval systems may be viewed as consisting of four major elements: input to the system, the file(s) that is (are) searched, searching methods, and output of the system. While each of these four elements is an essential part of any effective system, they are subject to differences in emphasis in various systems and there are differences in the theories and techniques that relate to them.

Traditional retrieval systems have put substantial efforts into the input stage on the theory that this would save work for the searcher. This reasoning has been challenged by some researchers who espouse the theory that less effort should be put into input, particularly when frequency of use of the system is relatively low, since the increased effort that this implies at the output end will not be significant because of the low frequency of use. The basis of this argu-

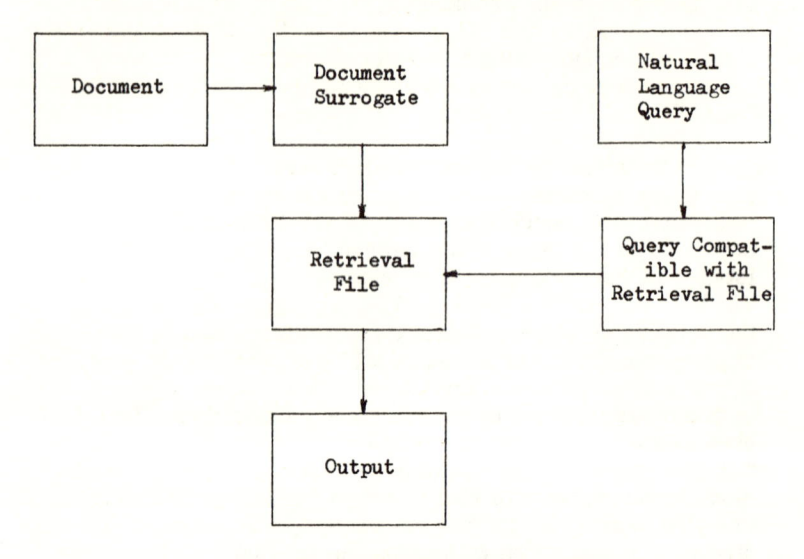

Figure 1. Document Retrieval System--General Model

ment is that while we have to index every document that enters the system, we will not necessarily wish to retrieve every document. One of the problems in this position is that the unit search cost which is cited usually includes only additional search time and does not include hidden costs resulting from loss of information, the non-retrieval of information that is available in the system but is not retrieved because of simplified, allegedly inexpensive, processing of documents for input.

An example of simplified input is the KWIC index, which is often difficult and time-consuming to search and has a relatively low retrieval performance. (Searching of the KWIC index is described in the section on searching.)

Some of the theories and techniques which relate to the four major system elements mentioned above will be discussed in detail later. However, some general comments can be made here concerning their role in the retrieval system. When we talk about input to the system we are concerned with those activities which relate to expressing the content of the document through the devices available for

Document Retrieval: General

this in the system.

The two steps involved here are:

(1) determining what the document is about and which part of its information content should be stored;

(2) translating the content to be stored into the intellectual and physical language of the system.

Either of these steps may be based either on human intellectual judgment applied to each document separately or on human judgment programmed for repeated execution by the machine.

Systems vary according to the nature and amount of skill needed for the steps indicated above, and the methods and devices available to perform them.

Preparation of materials for input may require intellectual or physical processing, or both.

The intellectual content of materials may be represented in a system in various ways: in its original form, whatever that may be; in the form of an abstract or an extract; through the use of an index language, or in some other way.

Representations of the intellectual content of documents may be entered into a system by using natural language or by the use of some kind of coding system. The differentiation between natural language tags and a code is made here in the sense in which the latter is used in the Dewey Decimal Classification, for example, to describe the subject content of a document.

Physical processing refers to those physical changes that materials must undergo to make them acceptable for input. In some cases physical processing must take place before intellectual processing, as in automatic indexing and abstracting methods in which the text to be indexed must be converted into machine readable form prior to processing. In other cases, as in some systems which involve the mechanical searching of stored document representations, conversion into machine readable form follows intellectual processing.

Systems vary in the specificity in which document content is described or in the potential specificity that may be achieved at the time of searching.

Referral from the document surrogate to the document itself is not necessary in systems in which the original materials are stored and retrieved along with the content representations or in those in which the original is the content representation. The latter is the case in mechanical full text searching, and in finding materials through browsing on library shelves, for example.

In some systems an identification or accession number is used to refer the user back to the original documents, and supplementary files must be searched to determine the documents' bibliographic address. Even further steps may be necessary to make their content available. Other systems may store the address and an abstract of the original along with the document surrogate.

The physical form in which document surrogates are stored may vary greatly, and may range all the way from something as conventional as a catalog card file, to be searched manually, to something as unconventional as magnetically recorded bits stored on tape or in quick access memory for computer searching. In between these there are many variations--microforms, punched cards, punched or magnetic tapes, printed lists, among others.

Another important characteristic of the file is its arrangement. Arrangement may mean that there is no arrangement, that items may be entered into the system at random, or it may mean rigidly intended order. Arrangement of the file is, of course, closely related to the searching method for which it is designed, as well as to the particular nature of the document representations.

The file (or files) to be searched may take many forms but its nature and its arrangement are characteristic of systems.

While the physical form of the document records in the retrieval file and the method of referral back to the original material are significant, it is also necessary to consider the absence, the presence, and the nature of synthesizing devices built into the arrangement of the file--which, in turn, may reflect similar devices which are part of the input

Document Retrieval: General

method. Synthesizing devices are intended to show relations between a network of document surrogates. A cross reference system is a familiar example of these devices.

Searching methods will be predetermined to a large extent by the nature of the document representations and by the characteristics of the file. In the final analysis the search strategies that are possible are greatly dependent on features built into the system.

Whenever a question is put to a system it must be formulated in terms of system characteristics, that is, it must be translated into the language of the system. Systems may be characterized by the amount of intellectual judgment they require and by the methods, tools, skills, etc., involved in this translation of inquiries into a language that the system can accept.

Other considerations are whether or not the subject tags included in the document representations are to be manipulated, whether that is desirable, and whether manipulation is of primary importance for a system. In coordinate indexing, except in the case in which a single term satisfies the inquiry, manipulation is indispensable.

A closely related consideration is the question whether the file remains intact during searching. A catalog drawer, for example, with a rod holding the cards, is a basically intact file; so is a printed bibliography. A deck of punched cards from which pertinent cards have been removed during searching is not an intact file. Cards must be re-filed in the deck before the next search is made if the same search is to give the same output. A "file" of books on a library's shelves is not intact because the books that are in circulation at any given time have been removed from it.

There are many variations in the steps involved between the immediate initial output and the final one in various systems. As was pointed out before, in some systems several steps are required to reach the final output. The immediate output may consist of a list of document accession numbers, for example, which lead only to the bibliographic address of the materials, and further steps are necessary to reach the final output.

The nature of the immediate initial output of the system and the steps that are or are not necessary to reach the final output are additional features that characterize systems.

One of the more discussed questions in documentation concerns the intellectual quality of output and the possibilities for influencing quality through various system features. This is also the question that is most difficult to answer satisfactorily, since the answer must be based on subjective judgment in some measure.

References

1. Artandi, Susan. "Document Description and Representation," In Annual Review of Information Science and Technology, Vol. 5. Chicago, Encyclopaedia Britannica, 1970. pp. 142-167.

2. Fairthorne, Robert A. "Essentials for Document Retrieval," Special Libraries, 46:340-353, October 1955.

3. Cleverdon, Cyril W., Jack Mills, and Michael Keen. Factors Determining the Performance of Indexing Systems. Vol. 1. Design. Cranfield, 1966, p. 40.

4. Maron, M. E. and Ralph M. Shoffner. The Study of Context: an Overview. Los Angeles, University of California, Institute of Library Research, 1969. (PB 183 329)

5. Benenfeld, Alan R., E. J. Gurley, and J. E. Rust. Cataloging Manual. ESL-TM-303. Cambridge, Mass., Massachusetts Institute of Technology, 1967.

CHAPTER 3

PROCESSING OF DOCUMENTS
FOR INPUT

Subject Indexing

Word Indexing

Index Languages

Lists of Terms

Pre-Coordination and Post-
Coordination

The Concept of Sets

Index Language Devices

Consistency of Indexing

Citation Indexing

SUBJECT INDEXING

Subject description as it is done by humans is a three-stage operation. First, the text of the document is scanned to determine its meaning, its information content. Second, a decision is made as to which parts of the document content are to be recorded in view of the objectives of the system. Third, the document content selected to be recorded is expressed in the language used in the system.[1]

It is obvious that deciding what the document is about and what of its content should be formally recognized for input to the retrieval system are complex intellectual operations. They involve considerable amount of subjective judgment that is influenced by such variables as the indexer's background; his understanding of the subject matter of the document; the objectives of the system and the needs of the users of the system; and the degree of effectiveness with which the author communicates his message to the indexer via the document.

The third step in the subject description, the formal recording of the selected document content, the "expression of aboutness," may be in the form of an abstract, an extract, index terms, or some other document surrogate. When descriptive tags are used, these may be in natural language or in some kind of a code. Natural language tags in turn may be controlled or uncontrolled.

DESCRIPTIVE TAGS

NATURAL LANGUAGE

controlled
or
uncontrolled

(index term
(descriptors
(subject headings
(etc.

CODES

controlled

(classification numbers
(other codes

Figure 2.

When a controlled vocabulary is used the third step in the subject description--expression of document content--involves the transformation of the subject content to be recorded into the formal, standardized, artificial language of the system. The indexer is presumably able to translate the selected subjects into a standard vocabulary because he understands both the document and the vocabulary. The process is essentially a matching procedure which involves the linking of two sets of words, the first set comprising the great variety of words that are used in the text of documents, and the second, a much smaller set of standard words which are designated as index terms. Equivalence between these two sets of terms is seldom made explicit. Usually the indexer must base his choice of index terms to describe the subject of the document on his own knowledge and judgment, and must apply some general rules of indexing related to the particular indexing system used. These rules may concern such things as specificity, preferred word forms, rules for number building in systems using numerical notation, or rules for citation order in pre-coordinate systems.

When there is no standardized vocabulary and the kind and level of the terms admitted to the system are not controlled, the indexer may use any word or words to describe the document without reference to any vocabulary or any previous indexing decisions. In this type of indexing the third step in the subject description is bypassed. The most severe consequence of lack of vocabulary control is the scattering of information under different synonyms, word forms, etc. Early coordinate indexing systems, for example, were based on uncontrolled vocabularies but it soon became evident that it was not efficient to dispense with subject authority or cross reference systems.[2]

While the question of controlled versus uncontrolled vocabularies is by no means resolved and while some new systems, such as Project Intrex, have no vocabulary control, the trend seems to be toward controlled vocabularies. This, in turn, raises the problem of convertibility of vocabularies in situations in which several data bases, each with its own controlled vocabulary, are used within a single organization. The choice then is either to search each data base separately for every query which requires the re-formulation of the query to make it compatible with each data base, or to merge the data bases into a single one. The latter approach requires the conversion of the various vocabularies into a common index language.

WORD INDEXING

In the foregoing, subject indexing was referred to as the procedure by which document content is expressed in the artificial language of the particular retrieval system used. While index languages will be discussed in detail in the unit which follows, it is useful to make the distinction here between system vocabulary and lead-in vocabulary because it helps to illustrate the difference between word indexing and subject indexing. The system vocabulary includes the terms under which entries may be made, terms which are actually used as index tags. The lead-in vocabulary of a system is an index referring from terms used in the literature to the terms in the system vocabulary.[3]

In word indexing, as in subject indexing with no vocabulary control, the system vocabulary is essentially the same as the lead-in vocabulary--that is, words are used as they are found in text to serve as index terms.

In word indexing words actually appearing in the titles, abstracts, or the full text of the documents are used as index terms. While the idea of word indexing is not new there is renewed interest in it in connection with current research in automatic indexing.

Crestadoro in 1856 published an account of word indexing from titles in his "Art of Making Catalogs," describing the application of the method to the catalog of the Manchester Free Public Libraries. The most widely known current example of word indexing from titles is the Key-Word-in Context or KWIC index, a machine-produced permuted title index. While there are variations in format, the KWIC index is essentially an alphabetical list of keywords occurring in the titles of the documents to be indexed. For each document there are as many entries in the index as there are keywords contained in it. Keywords are established indirectly by having the machine reject all words in the title that are included in a pre-determined list of non-significant words and list the remaining words as index terms. (See also unit on KWIC indexes.)

The limitations of word indexing are fairly obvious. A general limitation is the one which also applies to subject indexing with no vocabulary control, the scattering of information under different synonyms, word forms, etc. Another limitation relates to text which contains humanly identifiable subjects but does not contain words which when used as index terms would adequately describe these subjects.

A limitation that applies particularly to word indexing from titles stems from the uncertain value of titles for indexing purposes. To overcome the latter, authors have been encouraged to assign informative titles to their publications.

An example of a misleading title is "Treatment for Aging Typewriters" for an article on typewriter maintenance. The single useful keyword in this title is <u>typewriters,</u> and the article would be lost to people looking for documents concerned with maintenance in general. In a KWIC index

Processing Documents for Input

the article would be also indexed under treatment and aging, which would allow it to be retrieved by searchers who are concerned with these terms in a different context.

INDEX LANGUAGES

The total number of index tags available for use in the subject description of a document constitutes the index language of the system.

The functions of an index language are:

1. To substitute a formal language for a variety of expressions in natural language so that translation from natural language to the artificial language of the system obeys a set of rules and can be done more or less consistently;

2. To provide an organization of the vocabulary which would show the entire network of relations between terms.[4]

A controlled vocabulary of standard terms is used to replace the great variety of words used in documents. It is introduced partly for reasons of economy, to reduce the number of unique terms which have to be entered in the file of document representations. Its more important purpose is to standardize subject description by both indexer and searcher. A third reason for using a controlled vocabulary is to increase the probability that the inquirer will retrieve all those documents in the file that are relevant to his question and will retrieve few or ideally no documents that are not relevant.

Whenever a controlled vocabulary is used by the indexer to describe the content of a document, the index language becomes the means of communication in the indexer-to-system, user-to-system, and system-to-user communication chain. For this reason the quality of the index language is one of the more important factors governing the performance of retrieval systems. Inadequacy of the indexing vocabulary can lead to indexing omissions, indexing errors, inconsistencies and lack of exhaustivity of indexing. Since query formulation involves the indexing of the natural language query, the quality of the index language is equally important for that process as well.

Control, so far as an index language is concerned, means the control of such things as the specificity of terms, the size of the vocabulary, the relationship between terms, the relationship among words in compound terms, as well as substituting a single term for all its synonyms, and determining the form of a word to be used.

The control of the index terms is essentially a matter of establishing relations among words. The combination into single index terms of such words as grass and grasses, or sun and solar is concerned with grammatical relationships between words. The combination into a single index term of words with the same root goes further but is still concerned with relations revealed by spelling. The equation of synonyms, however, is concerned with semantic relationships, with words related by meaning.

Synonyms, in natural language, are words which have the same meaning. In information retrieval, however, near-synonyms are frequently treated as synonyms and are arbitrarily represented by a single index term. Synonyms are controlled by the designation of one paricular word to represent all of the synonymous terms as the accepted index term. See references are made from the synonyms not used in indexing to the term selected to represent them.

Variant word forms are usually represented by a single, preferred, form. The most common example of word form control is that of the singular and the plural forms of the same word, such as hydrocarbon and hydrocarbons. Sometimes word form control means the combination of adjectival and substantive forms (solar, sun), of participal and gerundive forms (printing, printed), or combining into one index term all words with the same root (extrusion, extruded, extrude, extruding).

Most systems do not limit the size of the vocabulary, although some are based on the concept of a small vocabulary. Even when a scheme attempts to limit its vocabulary, rules for its growth are usually made.

Index languages often display hierarchical relations among terms. These may be generic or non-generic. An example of the former is the genus/species relationship, such as the one between mammals and cow. A non-generic hierarchical relationship involves other relationships such as those between a thing and its parts, its processes, its prop-

Processing Documents for Input

erties, the operations performed on it, and so on. Examples are the relationship between ethyl alcohol and the synthesis of ethyl alcohol, or titanium and conductivity of titanium. In classification schemes, the display of generic relations may also display a coordinate relation among terms which are subordinate to the same term. For example, ethyl alcohol, methyl alcohol and butyl alcohol have a coordinate relation when they are subordinated to the same generic term, alcohols.

Specificity relates to the generic level of the index terms used and is defined as the degree to which the exact species rather than the containing genus is recognized. Depending on the specificity available in a particular index language, documents on cryogenic engineering would be indexed under Cryogenic Engineering or under Engineering.

Exhaustivity or depth of indexing refers to the degree to which the indexer recognizes (includes in the subject description) the different concepts and notions dealt with in the document. Exhaustivity is not dependent on the indexing vocabulary but is a decision of the indexer. Both specificity and exhaustivity were found to be important factors governing the performance of retrieval systems and they will be discussed from that point of view in the section on the evaluation of the performance of retrieval systems.

Citation order concerns the order of elements, whether expressed in words or in other notations, in a compound index term. This order is important in manual systems in which the number of file entries must be limited, because it has bearing on the information access points which are available in the system. Citation order would determine, for example, whether an article on computer programming would be indexed under Computers, programming or Programming, computers. In a system in which no provision is made for multiple access, the access point for the document would be Programming or Computers, depending on the particular citation order used.

The Universal Decimal Classification, for example, provides a standard citation order applicable whenever no strong argument exists for some other order. The standard order is: Whole thing - Kinds - Parts - Materials - Property - Processes - Operations - Agents. The use of plastic film for fruit barrels would be classified as: Fruit (whole thing) - Pulp (kind, according to state or condition) - Storage (operation) - <u>Barrels</u> (agent) - <u>Liners</u> (part of agent) - <u>Plastic</u> (material part of agent).[5]

John Metcalfe prefers the term "horizontal order of terms" to citation order and says that in alphabetic subject indexing,

> although opinions are conflicting, in most practices there is an order that seems fairly uniform in result...and seems fairly easily applied intuitively but not easily defined. It has been described as being from concrete to abstract; but in some sense the first and last terms may be concrete...it has also been described as being from most to least general or least to most specific.[6]

In faceted schemes, citation order is usually linked to the sequence of facets in the schedule. Usually, but not necessarily, the system rules specify that if facets ABCD are listed in that order in the schedule they should be combined to give an index heading in which the order of the element is ABCD. Since citation order is so closely linked to facet order, the selection of a helpful facet order becomes most important in these schemes. (Faceted schemes are discussed in greater detail in the section on Pre-coordination and Post-coordination.)

Ranganathan established a universal facet formula for the Colon Classification: Personality - Matter - Energy - Space - Time (P-M-E-S-T).[7] The British Classification Research Group developed a less rigid series of citation chains for their faceted classification schemes:

I. Entity - Part - Constituent

II. Entity - Property - Measure

III. Entity - Process

IV. Entity - Operation - Agent

LISTS OF TERMS

The index language of a system with a controlled vocabulary is codified in lists referred to as thesauri, subject heading lists, classification schedules, etc. These lists

Processing Documents for Input

are tools that indexers use in describing the content of documents in order that each may describe similar content consistently. They are also useful in the formulation of search instructions for improved retrieval because they help searchers to describe their information needs in the language used by the indexers. In addition to listing terms, thesauri usually include a set of rules for their application.

Several publications attempt to provide guidance for the compilation of thesauri; for example, the Guidelines for the Development of Information Retrieval Thesauri, prepared under the sponsorship of the Committee on Scientific and Technical Information (COSATI) of the Federal Council for Science and Technology; the DoD Manual for Building a Technical Thesaurus; and the Rules for Thesaurus Preparation published by ERIC. These include instructions concerning such things as term selection, the use of noun or adjectival form, singular versus plural, direct versus inverted entry, synonyms, quasi-synonyms, punctuation, and cross reference. [8,9,10]

Compilers of traditional classification schemes have started with a universe of knowledge, which they divided and subdivided to construct a classificatory tree, as in the Dewey Decimal Classification. Faceted schemes, instead of trying to construct one vast tree of knowledge, start with terms derived from the literature. Selected terms are grouped into such categories as: substance, state, property, reaction, operation, device, and so on, and are then organized into a classificatory array. Many thesauri come about through a rather unsystematic collection of terms arranged in some useful order. Terms may be listed in alphabetical, classified, or some other order, and a given thesaurus may contain the same terms arranged in several different orders. Elaborate cross referencing is often used in thesauri to display the different relationships that exist among the vocabulary terms.

Traditionally, thesauri have been viewed primarily as aids to the indexer in finding the correct term, and somewhat less attention has been paid to the use of the thesaurus as a searching aid. This seems to be changing and interest in the thesaurus as a searching aid has been increasing, particularly with reference to interactive systems in which display of the vocabulary is part of the user prompting apparatus. [11]

PRE-COORDINATION AND POST-COORDINATION

The kind of system in which terms are manipulated, combined, or coordinated at the time of searching is a post-coordinate system. The kind of system in which coordination is done at the time of indexing is a pre-coordinate system.

In <u>pre-coordinate systems</u> documents are searched under the same terms which the indexer originally assigned to them, without any further manipulation of terms at the time of searching. This means that whenever compound terms are used they are created at the time of indexing rather than at the time of searching. For example, a compound index term such as <u>Library automation</u> is created through the pre-coordination of the terms <u>Library</u> and <u>Automation.</u> In a pre-coordinate system the single index term <u>Library Automation</u> or <u>Automation, library,</u> etc. would be used and would serve as the search term for this particular subject.

There are a number of different pre-coordinate systems: <u>Enumerative schemes</u> enumerate the names of subjects of the terms which can be assigned to documents. Traditional enumerative schemes have been largely hierarchical. They have a "tree of knowledge" structure that begins with a universe of knowledge and then divides and subdivides it. In this kind of structure only two types of relations are expressed among terms: the generic relation of each lower term to the term above it and the coordinate relation among terms at the same hierarchical level. Any term is immediately subordinate to only one other term. The Dewey Decimal Classification and the Universal Decimal Classification are examples of this kind of enumerative hierarchical scheme even though they have many synthetic features.

In <u>synthetic schemes,</u> instead of trying to construct one vast tree of knowledge, schedules are constructed through facet analysis. Terms encountered in the literature of a given field are grouped into useful categories (facets) as: substance, state, property, operation, device and are arranged within each facet in some kind of hierarchical order.

In synthetic schemes pre-coordinate index terms are created through the combination of terms from different facets. The citation order of these compound terms is

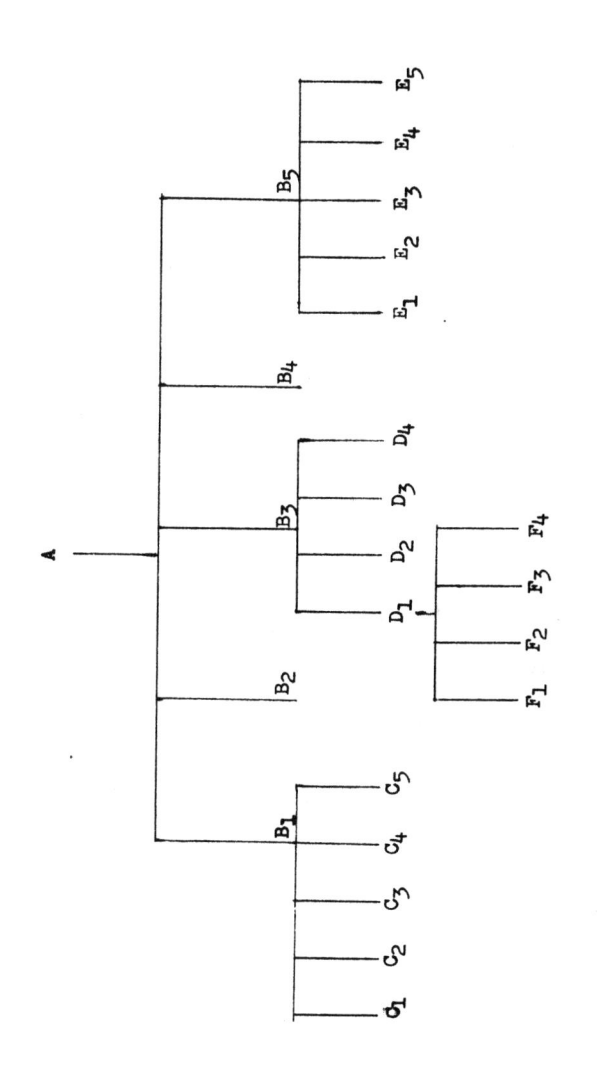

Figure 3. "Tree of Knowledge" Structure

linked to the order of the facets in the schedules.

For example, in the field of chemistry one could have the following facets and terms:

Facets	Terms
Substance	alcohol water air, etc.
State	liquid solid, etc.
Property	volatility melting point, etc.
Reaction	combustion condensation, etc.
Operation	analysis synthesis, etc.

A compound term to indicate that a document is about the volatility of liquid alcohol would be created by combining the appropriate terms from the different facets in the order which is suggested by the order of the facets in the schedules.

It was Ranganathan, in his Colon Classification,[7] who first developed the techniques of facet analysis and created the first basically synthetic scheme. His ideas were further developed and applied to a number of specialized subject fields by the British Classification Research Group. Synthetic schemes have had considerable influence on enumerative schemes. New editions of the Universal Decimal Classification and of the Dewey Decimal Classification show this influence. Facet analysis also has potential value for the index language builder, in that it offers a set of principles and techniques for vocabulary control.

Many pre-coordinate schemes are neither hierarchical nor synthetic, but merely consist of a vocabulary and a set of more or less rigid rules for indexing and vocabulary building. Whether a particular scheme does or does not use notation is immaterial so far as the basic logic of the scheme is concerned. Frequently, discussion in the literature of

Processing Documents for Input 47

schemes for classifying or otherwise organizing literature concentrates, erroneously, on notational features at the expense of a sound exposition of the logical structure of the schemes.

Post-coordinate systems were originally based on the assignment of unit-concept single-word terms (uniterms) to documents. These were to be coordinated at the time of searching in order to retrieve documents dealing with compound subjects. Thus, in a post-coordinate system, to use the previous example, Library and Automation would be the index terms assigned. If an inquiry related to library automation, then the file would be searched through the coordination of the two terms: Library and Automation. In other words, the universe of documents would be searched to determine which documents have both terms, Library and Automation, assigned to them.

The development of coordinate indexing is closely associated with Mortimer Taube, although he was preceded by others, including Batten in England and Cordonnier in France, in this approach to indexing.

When the method was first applied by Taube to organize a group of ASTIA (Armed Forces Technical Information Agency) documents, the system was to be based on a small vocabulary of single words taken from the text or titles of the documents indexed. These terms were all of equal value and no attempt was made at any kind of vocabulary control or cross reference systems or control of coordination of terms. Today's coordinate indexing systems gradually evolved from this early form.

Coordinate indexing systems no longer adhere rigidly to the idea that each index term must consist of a single word. Index terms made up of two or more words are frequently used and they are post-coordinated in searching in the same manner as single-word terms. These multiple word terms (polyterms) were introduced to cut down on the number of coordinations required in searching. They may be regarded as pre-coordinate terms which are post-coordinated in searching. This procedure is sometimes referred to in the literature as concept coordination.

Early coordinate indexing systems were based on inverted files (entry on term) both in their manual and machine applications. Today a number of large coordinate machine systems operate with a direct (serial) file (the MEDLARS system, for example) which can be updated relatively easily by merely adding new material to the end of the file. Computer based coordinate indexing systems can also be based on the combined use of a direct and an inverted file within a single system. For a discussion of Methods of file organization see the section on Retrieval of Documents.

Other changes and adaptations made over the years include the use of controlled vocabularies codified in thesauri. These include cross reference systems and frequently display hierarchical relationships among terms. The assumed advantage of free coordination--the almost unlimited possibility for the combination of terms--turned out in many cases to be disadvantageous. <u>Links</u> and <u>roles</u> had to be introduced to prevent unwanted coordinations. Links are intended to show that terms are related to each other, and roles are intended to show functional relationships between terms. (Links and roles are discussed in detail in the unit on Index Language Devices.)

THE CONCEPT OF SETS

Instead of viewing the indexing process as the assignment of descriptive tags to documents it is also possible to examine indexing as well as post-coordination in the context of set theory.

A set is a collection of objects called the elements of the set. There are two ways of describing a set: (1) by listing all the elements of the set, or (2) by describing a property which holds for all members of the set.

In document retrieval we deal with sets of documents that are described through the properties that hold for the documents in the collection. The particular property described may be the subject content of the document, its author(s), the journal in which the article was published, the language in which it was written, or some other characteristic.

Potentially a given document can have <u>membership</u> in a large number of different sets but, as far as a given retrieval system is concerned, the membership of a document is limited to those sets that are formally recognized in indexing. For example, a document on penicillin therapy, pub-

Processing Documents for Input 49

lished in 1965 by J. Smith, could be viewed as a member of the following sets, not all of which would necessarily be formally recognized by the indexer.

Set A = Documents on penicillin

Set B = Documents on therapy

Set C = Documents whose author is J. Smith

Set D = Documents published in 1965

Set E = Documents published in 1965 by J. Smith

Set F = Documents published in 1965 by J. Smith on penicillin

Set G = Documents published in 1965 by J. Smith on penicillin therapy

Set H = Documents published on penicillin in 1965

By assigning the three terms Penicillin, Therapy, and J. Smith to this document the indexer could formally recognize only sets A, B and C for the purpose of the retrieval system. Possible sets are formalized in the indexing vocabulary whenever controlled vocabularies are used.

Subsets

Several of the sets given above are subsets of another set because every element of the one set is also an element of the other. For example, Set E (documents published in 1965 by J. Smith) is a subset of Set D (documents published in 1965), as well as a subset of Set C (documents whose author is J. Smith); and Set G (documents published by J. Smith on penicillin therapy), is a subset of Set C (documents whose author is J. Smith). In fact, Set G is a subset of all of the sets listed above.

In other words, A is a subset of B. Every element of A has those properties which place it in B and, in addition, certain other properties which may distinguish its elements from those of B that do not belong to the elements of A.

In the above example, E is a subset of D because elements of E are documents published in 1965, which places E in D. However, the elements of E are documents published in 1965 by J. Smith, which distinguishes them from those elements of D which are documents published in 1965 whose author is other than J. Smith.

A set may also be described through the properties it does not have, for example, the set of documents by J. Smith that are not on penicillin.

Combination of Sets

The objective of searching is to select out of the universal set (all documents in the system) the particular set of documents that is specified by the query. In pre-coordinate systems the query is described through the sets that were created at the time of indexing. In post-coordinate systems (coordinate indexing) a given query may be described by sets that are different from those used orginally in indexing, through the combination of the original sets, involving the Boolean operators AND, OR, and NOT.

For example, let us assume that the following sets were originally created in indexing:

    Set A = Documents on aspirin
             (Contains documents D_1, D_3, D_5)

    Set B = Documents on allergy
             (Contains documents D_2, D_4, D_5, D_6)

    Set C = Documents by James Brown
             (Contains documents D_7, D_8)

    Set D = Documents on therapeutic effects
             (Contains documents D_1, D_9, D_{10})

Out of these original sets a new set could be created to satisfy the query, "What documents deal with the therapeutic effects of aspirin?"

In this example the query calls for a set of documents that was not created in indexing, i.e. documents dealing with the therapeutic effects of aspirin. However, in a post-coordinate system a set can be defined through the combination of two original sets using the Boolean operator AND to combine sets A and D. The set that will satisfy the query is A AND D (sometimes written AD)--the set of documents that belong to both set A and set D. In other words, the query calls for documents that have the indexing terms Aspirin and Therapeutic effects both assigned to them. These should be documents about the therapeutic effects of aspirin--a subject that is more specific than the subjects represented by either of the original terms.

In addition to the AND operator, the use of the NOT operator also results in a set that represents a subject that is more specific than the subjects represented by each of the combined sets alone. For example, D and NOT A (DA), therapeutic effects except for the therapeutic effects of aspirin, is a more specific subject than either therapeutic effects or aspirin alone.

When two sets are combined through the Boolean connective OR, in an inclusive sense the resulting set represents a subject that has the same specificity or is less specific than the subjects represented by either of the combined sets. A or B in the above example means the set of documents dealing with aspirin or allergy, or both.

Venn diagrams help to visualize the relationships just described. In Figure 4 the rectangle represents the universal set (all documents in the retrieval system) and the two intersecting circles represent set A and set B respectively.

It should be noted that the use of Boolean operators is not limited to two sets or to a single operator within a given function. Complex Boolean functions, including many terms and several operators, can be used to describe a set of documents that will satisfy a given query. The large number of combinations that are theoretically possible is, however, limited in practice by the intellectual limitations imposed by the subject matter of the document collection and by the operational limitations imposed through system design.[12]

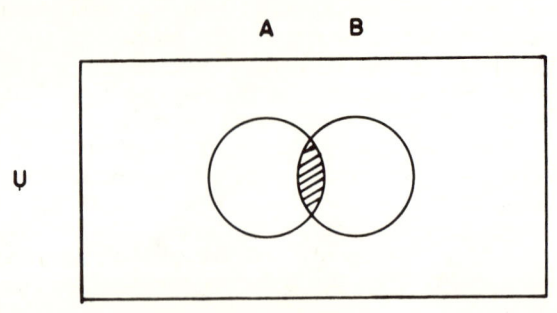

Shaded area represents AB (A *and* B)

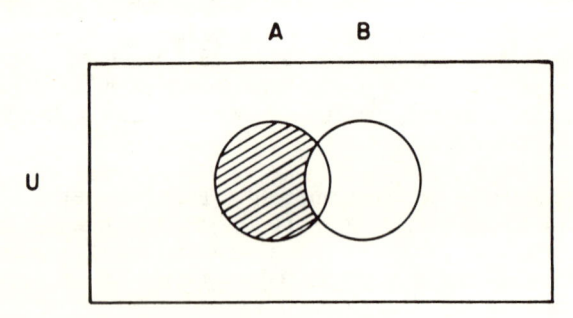

Shaded area represents A$\overline{\text{B}}$ (A *and not* B)

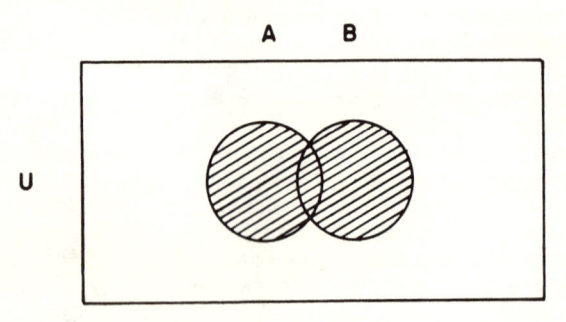

Shaded area represents A+B (A *or* B)

Figure 4.

Processing Documents for Input

INDEX LANGUAGE DEVICES

Cleverdon suggests that indexing systems are made up of a basic vocabulary together with a number of devices. These devices fall into two main categories: 1) recall devices which are intended to increase the probability of retrieving a larger number of relevant documents, and 2) precision devices which are intended to ensure that non-relevant documents are not retrieved.[13] Precision devices increase the specificity of terms and recall devices have the opposite effect of making terms broader.

Precision devices are the following:

Coordination - the conjunction of two or more terms to produce a narrower class defined by their intersection; e.g. Computer and Processing to give Computer Processing.

Weighting - the assignment to a term of a figure representing the relative significance of that term in the total subject description of the document. Thus, a term which represents a central theme in the document gets a high weighting, and one which represents only a marginal element in the subject content of the document gets a low weighting. A term with a weight assigned to it is more specific than the same term without a weight. For example, Penicillin with a weight of 2 is more specific than Penicillin because it represents a subset of the penicillin set.

Links - indicating particular connection between two or more terms, where the lack of such a link might create ambiguity. For example, if the same document deals with the hardness of copper and the conductivity of titanium, a link between Hardness and Copper on the one hand, and between Conductivity and Titanium on the other, would avoid combination of Hardness and Titanium or Conductivity and Copper, and would ensure that each property refers only to the subject with which it is actually linked in the article.

Roles - indicating the function of a particular term in an indexing description.

Recall devices are the following:

Confounding synonyms - accepting items indexed by X when searching for Y, that is, treating X and Y as if they were synonymous.

Confounding word forms - accepting items indexed by different forms of the search term such as its singular, plural, participal, or gerund.

In systems with controlled vocabularies where confounding of synonyms and word forms is done at the time of indexing, confounding in searching applies primarily to near synonyms.

Generic and non-generic hierarchical linkage - accepting items indexed by terms which are in some hierarchical relation to the search term. For example, the class Cooling might be extended hierarchically to include the subordinate term Sweat Cooling, the superordinate term Heat Transfer, the coordinate term Heating, and the collateral term Radiation.

The ways in which index language devices can be used in searching will be described in the unit on searching.

The function of roles and links is illustrated by the following example from Mortimer Taube.[14] If one has a document on lead as a coating material and another document on coatings for lead, and if the system has terms for only lead and coating, then the system will deliver noise. Suppose the first document's accession number is 100 and that of the second is 101. Then, in accordance with the inverted form, there would be the following postings:

Lead	Coating
100	100
101	101

Both documents would be retrieved as an answer to a question concerned with lead used as a coating material. Since only document 100 deals with lead as coating, 50% of the documents retrieved would not be relevant to the inquiry.

The use of roles in this case would eliminate noise by breaking up the single lead class into several, such as lead, lead as a product, lead as a raw material, and so on.

To illustrate the use of links Taube uses the example of a document on the subject "lead coatings for copper pipes." In a system which uses no links or roles the document would be indexed under the following terms:

Processing Documents for Input   55

Lead	Coating	Copper	Pipes
100	100	100	100

To an inquiry on lead pipes this document would be retrieved through false coordination between <u>Lead</u> and <u>Pipes</u>. This can be avoided by linking <u>Lead</u> and <u>Coating</u>, and <u>Copper</u> and <u>Pipes</u> through the use of additional symbols in the following manner:

Lead	Coating	Copper	Pipes
100A	100A	100B	100B

However, while this will eliminate the possibility of a false coordination between <u>Lead</u> and <u>Pipes</u>, it will also make impossible a potentially useful coordination between <u>Coating</u> and <u>Pipes</u> to answer an inquiry about "coatings for pipes." The same would be true of a document dealing with "penicillin therapy for aspirin allergy." Linking <u>Penicillin</u> with <u>Therapy</u> and <u>Aspirin</u> with <u>Allergy</u> would make impossible the potentially useful coordination of <u>Allergy</u> with <u>Therapy</u>.

Thus a system of links which effectively rules out noise may also rule out relevant information.

A number of coordinate indexing systems--the Engineers Joint Council system, for example--developed elaborate systems of roles and links. Other systems operate without links and roles.

While they are more easily applied in a subject field whose language is precise and reasonably unambiguous, roles are generally difficult to apply consistently, and their use tends to increase the complexity of the indexing process as well as the process of query formulation. Indexing time and cost of indexing are also increased. The trend seems to be away from roles because they are frequently not judged effective enough to justify the cost involved in their application. This point of view was reinforced by the MEDLARS evaluation study which showed that less than 10% of the false coordinations would have been prevented through the use of roles. Instead of roles the study recommends the use of more specific terms.[15]

CONSISTENCY OF INDEXING

An important but far from adequately understood problem related to human indexing is inter- and intra-indexer consistency. This concerns the relative priority indexers assign to index terms associated with a given document, and the extent of agreement on such assignment among different indexers or the same indexer at different times.

The quality of indexer performance has been traditionally linked with consistency and a high degree of consistency has been generally viewed as a desirable objective in indexing.

At the same time it has been suggested that consistency per se is a meaningless objective, that it is of interest only if there is a relationship between the consistency obtained under a given indexing method and the level of retrieval performance achieved, and that we need to know more about this relationship before indexer consistency can be safely used as a gauge of indexing quality.[16]

Indexer consistency is measured on the basis of agreement or lack of agreement of indexers on the terms they assign to the same document.[17]

The relatively few studies which have been made of consistency of indexing found it to be generally low. A study of government information agencies, for example, showed that within an individual agency, consistency in applying the same subject terms to a document when it is re-indexed is low, ranging from 62 to 72 percent. Other studies are concerned with the effect on consistency of such variables as indexing experience, the length of documents, and the depth of indexing.[18]

A University of Chicago study deals with such crucial questions as: When indexers assign different terms to a document, and are considered inconsistent, what is the nature of this inconsistency? To what extent do these inconsistent terms differ from each other? To what extent do they reflect different views on the level of specificity? Does the degree of indexing inconsistency differ with depth of indexing?[19]

Many questions, however, remain unanswered by

these studies. An important question concerns the effect of free versus controlled vocabularies on consistency of indexing. In the case of controlled vocabularies, the optimum degree of control and the particular method of thesaurus organization which would result in the greatest probability for consistency remain to be established.

In automatic indexing, the type of indexing where human interpretation and judgment do not play a repeated role in the indexing of each document, problems of inconsistency do not exist. While a variety of automatic indexing methods are in existence it is generally true of all these methods that as long as the same algorithm is applied to the same text, the same indexing will result.

CITATION INDEXING

While citation indexing is not subject analysis in the sense in which it was discussed earlier, the method is intended to provide subject access to documents. Citation indexing is based on the assumption that bibliographic citations are useful clues to the subject content of documents.

The citation index is a list of references, each accompanied by a list of documents which have cited it. The user must begin his search with at least one specific known document on the subject he is interested in. When this known document is looked up, the citation index will give a list of all citing documents which are within the scope of the index and which have been cited within the time period set by the index. Thus, from this starting point one may find citations forward in time to subsequent papers related to earlier papers, and citations in citing papers can be used as new known documents. This process is called forward cycling and can be continued until you run out of citing papers.

Going backward in time, backward cycling, simply means looking up items in the bibliography of an article, then doing the same for each item in the bibliographies of the found items, and so on. This type of use of citations has been common with scholars for many years and it can be done directly from the documents themselves, with no need for an index of any type.

An attractive feature of citation indexes is that their preparation does not require indexers trained in specialized fields. Indexing is a purely clerical procedure, based entirely on the citations accompanying documents, and does not involve complex judgments concerning subject content and the evaluation of this content in terms of its preservation for future retrieval. Because citation indexing is a purely clerical procedure it easily lends itself to mechanization.

Some questions relating to this method of indexing are the following: How correct is the assumption that inquiries related to specific subjects can be satisfactorily answered through the citation index? How does the performance of a citation index compare with that of a subject index? Do citation indexes take the place of subject indexes, or should they be considered supplementary to them? How valid are some of the claims related to the usefulness of citation indexing?

In order to be able to discuss the value of citation indexing one must examine the role and nature of citations and the correlation between the citations used by the author and the subject of the article. Citations may or may not be part of a bibliography for a variety of reasons. Citation in a bibliography may have been used to document a procedure or a statistical process which has little to do with the subject of the paper. Exclusion may come about through editorial policy, and inclusion may come about for reasons of prestige, availability, or ignorance of other more relevant papers. There is also the problem of non-citation. Articles which are not cited or articles which are not cited within a short time after their publication will be lost for the period when they could make their greatest impact. Also, the chances of a paper being cited will vary according to whether the paper was published early or late in the period of time covered by the citation index. For example, an article published at the beginning of a twelve-month span will have a greater chance of being cited than one published at the end of this period.

One of the more important claims made for a citation index is that it can function as a subject index, and is, indeed, superior to subject indexes for retrieval of documents on a subject.[20] Two fairly recent studies shed some light on the potential and limitations of the citation index. One study found that the citation index is less effective than subject indexing in the retrieval of relevant documents for a given inquiry. In searching of the citation index, noise increased with each step. The only ratio in which the citation index scored higher than the subject index was the recall ratio, which seems to suggest its usefulness as a complementary tool, to retrieve additional material.[21]

Another study was concerned with the preparation of a bibliography on the drug thalidomide, using Chemical Abstracts and Index Medicus, as compared with a similar bibliography prepared through the search of the Science Citation Index. In this case it was concluded that the two types of indexes could be used profitably together; each produced a large number of references not found in the other. For the particular search used in the experiment the Science Citation Index was not appreciably less efficient as a retrieval tool than were Chemical Abstracts and Index Medicus; for short-time intervals it was more efficient.[22]

While these and other studies related to citation indexing are interesting and useful, it is clear that more extensive studies are needed to determine the usefulness of citation indexing as compared with subject indexing.

There are at least two uses of the citation index in which it has a unique value: determining the impact value of a given document, and finding criticism of published experimental results. If many references have been made to a paper it would appear that it has had significant impact in the field; to find criticism of a paper one can examine citing articles listed in the citation index.

An experimental approach to subject access through citations is bibliographic coupling. This method assumes that when two (or more) documents have common references, they have subject matter in common. The strength of the subject relationship is determined by the number of common references.

A group of researchers at the University of California have been experimenting with objective criteria other than citations as a means of describing the content of documents. They introduced the concept of "context" which, in contrast with "content," means external, measurable attributes and relationships of a document. Examples of context information for a document are the journal in which it was published, the papers it cites, the reviews that appeared about it, and the journals in which the reviews were published. It is hypothesized that context information provides direct clues to the content of the document and that there is a relationship between context and content.[23]

References

1. Vickery, Brian C. On Retrieval System Theory. 2nd ed. London, Butterworths, 1965.

2. Artandi, Susan and Theodore C. Hines. "Roles and Links, or Forward to Cutter," American Documentation, 14:74-77, January 1963.

3. Cleverdon, Cyril W., Frederick W. Lancaster, and Jack Mills. "Uncovering Some Facts of Life in Information Retrieval," Special Libraries, 55:86-91, February 1964.

4. Gardin, Jean Claude, cited by Eric de Grolier in: On the Theoretical Basis of Information Retrieval Systems. Final Report to the Air Force Office of Scientific Research Under Contract AF61(052)-505. Paris, 1965, p. 6.

5. Mills, Jack. The Universal Decimal Classification. Vol. I. Rutgers Series on Systems for the Intellectual Organization of Information. Susan Artandi, ed. New Brunswick, N.J., Graduate School of Library Service, Rutgers-The State University, 1964, p. 50.

6. Metcalfe, John. Alphabetical Subject Indication of Information. Vol. III. Rutgers Series on Systems for the Intellectual Organization of Information. Susan Artandi, ed. New Brunswick, N.J. Graduate School of Library Service, Rutgers-The State University, 1965. pp. 101-102.

7. Ranganathan, S.R. The Colon Classification. Vol. IV. Rutgers Series on Systems for the Intellectual Organization of Information. Susan Artandi, ed. New Brunswick, N.J. Graduate School of Library Service, Rutgers-The State University, 1965.

8. Committee on Scientific and Technical Information. Federal Council for Science and Technology. Guidelines for the Development of Information Retrieval Thesauri. Draft. Washington, D.C. Office of Sci-

ence and Technology, Executive Office of the President, November 9, 1966.

9. Project LEX, Office of Naval Research. DoD Manual for Building a Technical Thesaurus. April 1966, ONR-25.

10. ERIC. Rules for Thesaurus Preparation. Washington, D.C., U.S. Government Printing Office. 1969.

11. Artandi, Susan. "Document Description and Representation." In: Annual Review of Information Science and Technology, Vol. 5. Chicago, Encyclopaedia Britannica, 1970. pp. 143-168.

12. Artandi, Susan. "Document Retrieval and the Concept of Sets," Journal of the American Society for Information Science, 22:289-290, July-August 1971.

13. Cleverdon, Cyril W. "The Cranfield Tests on Index Language Devices," Aslib Proceedings, 19:173-194, June 1967.

14. Taube, Mortimer. "Notes on the Use of Roles and Links in Coordinate Indexing," American Documentation, 12:98-100, April 1961.

15. Lancaster, Frederick W. "On the Need for Role Indicators in Post-Coordinate Retrieval Systems," American Documentation, 19:42-46, Jan. 1968.

16. Cooper, William S. "Is Interindexer Consistency a Hobgoblin?" American Documentation, 20:268-278, July 1969.

17. Zunde, Pranas and Margaret E. Dexter. "Indexing Consistency and Quality," American Documentation, 20:259-267, July 1969.

18. St. Laurent, M. C. A Review of the Literature of Indexer Consistency. M.A. thesis, University of Chicago Graduate Library School, 1967.

19. Swanson, Don R. Studies of Indexing Depth and Retrieval Effectiveness. Progress Report No. 1. The University of Chicago Graduate Library School, 1966.

20. Garfield, Eugene. "Citation Indexes for Science," Science, 122:108-111, July 15, 1955.

21. Huang, Theodore S. "Efficacy of Citation Indexing in Reference Retrieval," Library Resources & Technical Services, 12:415-434, Fall 1968.

22. Spencer, Carol C. "Subject Searching With Science Citation Index: Preparation of a Drug Bibliography Using Chemical Abstracts, Index Medicus, and Science Citation Index, 1961 and 1964," American Documentation, 18:87-96, April 1967.

23. Maron, M. E. and Ralph M. Shoffner. The Study of Context: an Overview. Los Angeles, University of California Institute of Library Research, 1969. (PB 183 329)

Chapter 4

THE RETRIEVAL OF DOCUMENTS

The File of Document Representations

Searching

Evaluation of Retrieval Systems

THE FILE OF DOCUMENT REPRESENTATIONS

After indexing is completed an index record for each document is created which contains document specifications (and location) and document description. Document description may consist of subject description only (index terms which were assigned) or may also include other information about the document.

A set of these individual records with common structural elements constitutes a retrieval file. The file is created by grouping records according to some organizational rule. The objective is to facilitate searching, that is, to help isolate a defined subset of records pertaining to an inquiry by stating the attributes of the records sought. The statement of attributes is called a query.

The organization of a file implies the specification of its information content (data contained in the records), the sequence of its records relative to each other, and the characteristics of the storage medium in which the file is stored.[1] Design of each of these aspects of the file is influenced by a number of factors external to the file, several of which are determined by patterns of use. Examples of factors influencing file design are access load (peak, average), response time required, desired reliability, rate of change, size and rate of growth, life span, categories of users and the type of access they need, frequency of use, and the amount of money available.

Records consist of fields which are arbitrarily designated to include certain elements of the records' content. One can arbitrarily designate on a catalog card, for example, the following fields: author, title, imprint, and subject. If desired, more fields may be created by breaking down the imprint field into separate fields for the publisher, place and date.

The particular way in which fields and data elements are arranged in a record will determine the record's format. Thus, it is useful to differentiate between the substantive content of a record and its format. In the case of an index record, for example, the substantive content of the record is determined by the indexer, while its format will depend on the storage medium used and the type of access required.

The Library of Congress cataloging record is an example of a record in which identical content is made available in at least two different formats: in printed form, and in binary form on magnetic tape (MARC).

In machine processing the format of a record serves as a basis for the location and identification of fields and data elements in the record, that is, it makes it possible to access the record's content. Since the machine does not "understand" the content of a record it identifies a particular piece of information within the record through its position or its relative position to some other piece of information.

Unless randomly arranged, a file is usually sequenced according to one or more of the fields contained in its records. The field or fields used for sequencing a file depend on which are considered most desirable access points for the purposes for which the file is to be used. The dictionary catalog, for example, is arranged in a single sequence according to three different fields--author, subject, and title. A classified catalog is sequenced on a single field, the classification number.

The main sequencing field used in a file is called the primary sort key. The field used to determine relative position among a set of records when the primary sort key has the same value for each record in the set is called a sub-

Retrieval of Documents 65

ordinate sort key. For example, when the primary sort key is the subject and items are filed alphabetically by author under the subject, then the author's name is the secondary sort key.

File Structures

A retrieval file is intended to link document descriptions with the items described. The set of links between terms and items can be displayed in the following two-dimensional matrix:

```
    Terms
Items \   A   B   C   D   E   F   G   -   -   -
      1   x       x           x
      2       x               x
      3           x   x           x
      4   x                   x
      5   x           x   x
      6   x   x
      7               x       x
      8           x           x   x
```

Figure 5. Term/Document Matrix

The matrix helps to illustrate two principal types of structures used in document retrieval files. When the matrix is read horizontally it is organized by items, with the terms arranged subordinately under the items (direct file). When read vertically, the sort key becomes the term and the items become the subordinate part of the file (inverted file).

In an inverted file the number of records should theoretically equal the number of terms used in the system. In direct files the records should equal the number of documents represented in the file.

Both types of files exist in both manual and machine forms and there are machine systems that use a combination of both.[2]

While manual coordinate indexing systems use inverted files, in machine based coordinate indexing systems the particular file structure used depends to a large extent on the storage medium involved. Magnetic tape systems are based predominantly on direct files, and inverted files are used with magnetic disk storage.

File structure as it was just described should be distinguished from file sequence. Records within either type of file structure can be sequenced in various ways, according to some logic or randomly.

Sequential order means that, based on the logic of the file, the nth record in the file will be followed by the nth+1 record. In a telephone directory, for example, the logical sequence is alphabetical and each record is followed by the one which is the next in the alphabetical array. Sequential arrangement is simple except for the problem of inserting new records between the existing ones. This requires moving all records which are beyond the point at which interfiling is necessary. The degree of difficulty will depend on the physical form of the file. For example, interfiling is relatively easy in a card catalog but it requires reprinting of the book catalog.

Sequential order should not be confused with sequential access. Records in files with sequential access, such as in magnetic tape files, may be arranged in a variety of ways and sequential access merely means that in order to reach a particular record it is necessary to go through all records preceding it in the file. This is in contrast with random access, in which it is possible to go directly to any place in the file. In random access the time required to reach any given record is, for all practical purposes, constant. (See also the section on Storage Devices.)

The technique of file organization that uses information in one record to locate the next record to be consulted, which is in some other part of the file, is called chaining. See and See also references are conventional examples of chaining.

In computer systems chaining is used when there is some reason for not placing the referenced record contiguous to the referring record. Reasons for this may be that one part of the storage device may be full while another part has empty space, or that it is too costly to interleave new records in their proper sequence.

File Processes

A file process is a transformation of a file which may involve the altering of individual records in the file or the altering of such things as the sequence, structure, and size of the file.

File processes of importance in document retrieval are _searching_, _sorting_, _merging_, and _file maintenance_.

Sorting is a file process which places the records in the file into a predetermined sequence according to some logic. In merging we start with two or more files, each in sequence by the same keys, and combine these into a single file. The number of records in the merged file will be equal to the sum of the number of records in the individual files. In manual systems merging corresponds to what is referred to as interfiling. Deleting of unwanted records may be considered as a negative merge where the resulting file is smaller than the original file. Both sorting and merging result in a change of the relative position of the records in the file.

Since the objective of searching is to identify those records in the file that match the criteria defined by the query it does not result in a transformation of the file unless the selected records are physically removed from the file.

File maintenance refers to a collection of file processes including the ones described above, and may involve some of the following: adding a record to the file, deleting a record from a file, changing a field in a record, changing the format of a record, changing the sequence of the records in the file, and changing the storage medium in which the file is stored.

SEARCHING

The searching procedure is essentially a communication process in which the nature of the question and the features inherent in the system affect search parameters. The objective of searching is to identify those documents in the collection which may satisfy a request for information. Or, to put it in Fairthorne's terms, the purpose is

> the recovery from a given collection of documents, with stated probability, a set of documents that includes, possibly with some irrelevant ones, all documents of specified content; or, a set of documents that includes nothing but documents of specified contents, but possibly not all of them.[3]

The success of matching the contents of the documents to the requested information will depend on some a priori conditions since the nature of the file searched is determined when the retrieval system is established. In other words, possible search strategies will be limited by features built into the system through design and implementation.

There is an interrelationship between searching methods and the characteristics of the document representations. The same is true of searching methods and the arrangement of the file. The particular nature of the document content representations will limit information access points and flexibility in searching. The overall match between the content of the file and the subject of the query will also influence search strategies and success in searching. In other words, allowing for some variation according to the skill of the individual searcher, both in terms of content and flexibility in searching, only that can be taken out of a system which was built into it.

A system may be designed to permit, to greater or lesser degree, such things as searching at various hierarchical levels. This would open or close classes to broaden or narrow the subject of the search. As a result, it would include or exclude related subjects, and would increase or decrease the specificity of the search as required. While a number of the possibilities just mentioned are applicable to many systems, there are vast differences in the number and kind of devices that are used in any particular system to accomplish them. A variety of techniques can be employed to provide for a similar degree of search flexibility. Part of the skill of the good searcher is knowing the characteristics of the system so that he can formulate search strategies in terms of those characteristics.

Query Formulation

When the searcher acts as an intermediary between the inquirer and the retrieval system he must try to satisfy the user, who is very likely to present his inquiry in terms of his own particular point of view. Another user will ask for the same information in a different way, and the information needs of the same user may vary from one occasion to another. It is very likely that the question will not be stated clearly initially and that discussion and clarification of subject matter will be necessary. Clarification here implies more than clarification of subject matter. Such things as the level at which, and the point of view from which, the information is sought must be considered. Then there is a value judgment required to decide whether it is preferable to retrieve a maximum number of relevant documents in the collection at the cost of retrieving some non-relevant ones, or whether it is desirable to reduce the number of non-relevant documents retrieved and to take the risk of not retrieving certain relevant ones. The former situation may be preferred in a patent search, while the latter would be preferable when only a few representative documents are sought. Depending on what is needed, the searcher must decide whether his search should result in a high recall ratio or a high precision ratio.

This type of question negotiation and subsequent query formulation have a significant effect on the performance of retrieval systems; indeed, it is being increasingly realized that the operations of indexing, vocabulary building and query formulation are highly interrelated procedures, and that a good system design should provide for their meaningful integration.[4] Qualitatively, query formulation includes the operation of indexing since it involves the indexing of the question. It is very much of an indexing problem and many of the complexities of indexing apply to it. Lack of understanding of the question, inadequate knowledge of system parameters and system vocabulary can lead to unsatisfactory query formulations, which in turn will cause output failures. Omission of appropriate terms from a query can lead to recall failures, and the use of inappropriate terms can cause precision failures.

Query formulation involves several steps. It begins with an information request described in natural language. When this is indexed the result is a list of terms to be matched against the retrieval file. Frequently, Boolean relationships are also specified for the query terms. In machine systems an additional step involves the structuring of the query to make it compatible with particular system requirements.

The following is an example of the three steps just described:

Step 1. <u>Natural language query</u>

What is the pattern of use of computers in libraries?

Step 2. <u>Indexing of query</u>

Terms: Use patterns (A)

Computers (B)

Libraries (C)

Boolean formulation: ABC (A AND B AND C)

Step 3. <u>Making the query compatible with system requirements</u>

If the TEXT-PAC* system were used, for example, the following format would be required:

A_1 USE ADJ PATTERNS

A_2 COMPUTERS

A_3 LIBRARIES

CON^1 A_1 AND A_2 AND A_3

---

*IBM Corporation. TEXT-PAC, S/360 Normal Text Information Processing, Retrieval, and Current Information Selection System. (360D-06.7.020)

Retrieval of Documents

Feedback

Search strategy is formulated by taking into consideration the characteristics of the index language used in a system, the characteristics of the file to be searched, and the mechanical capabilities which are present in the system; adjustments and changes in search strategy are made in response to feedback from the system. Various systems, depending upon their design have the capability of providing more or less feedback to indicate what the system offers on a given subject. Depending on what is found during the search, feedback enables the searcher to adjust the search strategy to produce the desired results. Feedback may indicate that an entirely different strategy ought to be tried, or that the problem should be approached from a different point of view. In a great number of systems, detection of feedback and its interpretation in terms of search strategy are based on the searcher's judgment. It is also possible to provide automatic feedback in a system through some quantitative criteria. Most computer based systems, for example, will tell the searcher the number of postings for each term in the query.

A relatively frequent adjustment is the broadening or narrowing of the scope of the search. A search can be broadened by expanding the original search instruction through the addition of terms which are in some kind of hierarchical relationship with the original search term. If, for example, the term Alcohol were added to the search term Ethyl Alcohol, a generic hierarchical relation would be explored. A non-generic hierarchical relation is used, for example, when the term Ethyl Alcohol is accepted as an additional search term in a search on synthesis of ethyl alcohol. The scope of the search can also be broadened by treating synonyms, near-synonyms, or similar word forms as equivalents.

In systems which have controlled vocabularies the control of synonyms and word forms is displayed in the index language. Synonyms are controlled by the designation of one particular synonym to be used as the accepted index term, and by the use of see references to refer from other synonyms to the accepted one. Word forms are usually combined to be represented by a single preferred form. A most common example of this is the control of the plural and the singular forms of the same term, such as Hydrocarbons and Hydrocarbon. Near-synonyms and related subjects may be indicated in a file through see also references or they may be left to the searcher to figure out and explore.

The scope of the search can be narrowed and its precision increased through coordination. Combination of terms creates a narrower class; as, for example, when the words School and Libraries are combined to make School libraries. A search can be narrowed by exploiting reversed hierarchical relationships and through the consideration of roles, links, and weights. Ignoring these will result in the broadening of the search.

System Characteristics and Search Strategies

The examples which follow are intended to show how system characteristics can influence the formulation of search strategies.

KWIC (Key-Word-In-Context) indexes usually have no vocabulary control. (A description of the KWIC index is given in the section on Representative Machine Applications.) The only definite information that is commonly available about the index language is a list of those terms which are not acceptable to the system. This is the opposite of what the searcher usually knows about a system, since customarily he is informed, through a subject heading list, a thesaurus, or a classification schedule, about those terms which are to be used, and instructed on how acceptable index terms can be created. Thus, in a KWIC index the searcher must work with index terms which are identical with the words appearing in the natural language title of the document. Since there is no vocabulary control, in order to do an exhaustive search he will have to search under all possible synonyms and all of the word forms that he can think of. Since there is no hierarchical structure or cross reference system in the file, it will be the searcher's job to remember the hierarchically or otherwise related terms if he is to find material that is in the index under any of the possible terms and is hidden by the accident of language usage. He will be able to use coordination by scanning the context around the key word to discover that it appears in combination with another word or words in the title. He may consider or disregard links and roles in the same way. The searcher receives almost no guidance from the system and he must depend on his own initiative and his familiarity with the terminology of the subject field being searched.

If the required information were concerned with "extrusion of polyethylene films," the following terms, among others, would have to be considered in searching a KWIC index:

Synonyms: Polyethylene, Polythene, Ethylene Polymer

Word Forms: Film, Films, Ethylene Polymer, Ethylene Polymers

Word Forms with Common Roots: Extrusion, Extruded, Extrude, Extruding

Non-generic Hierarchical Relationship (with extrusion): Manufacture, Fabrication, etc.

Generic Hierarchical Relation (with Polyethylene): Polyolefines, Thermoplastics, Plastics, Synthetic Polymers, Polymers

Coordination: By specifying, for example, that both Polyethylene (or its appropriate substitute term) and Extrusion (or its appropriate substitute term) should appear in the title.

Links: By requiring not only the above but also that Extrusion should refer to Polyethylene in the title (and not to some other material which may also appear in the title).

Chemical Abstracts subject indexing uses a flexible controlled vocabulary. Such things as synonyms, word forms, common roots, are controlled with emphasis on the main heading, rather than the modifying phrases. Chemical Abstracts follows the policy of highly specific indexing and only very general articles are indexed under generic terms:

Synonyms: Because of the synonym control it is not necessary to search under all possible synonyms; only the particular one used is to be located and all material will be listed under it. See references are provided to lead the searcher from synonyms that are not used to the term used.

Word forms, Common Roots, etc.: These are also controlled and one form is usually designated to be used as the index term. There may or may not be see references from forms that are not used to the word forms that are used, and familiarity with the system and the terminology of the field helps in the location of the right term for searching.

Hierarchical Relationships: These are not displayed in the file; materials are indexed under the specific term. Moving to the hierarchically higher term will not result in the complete expansion of the class because only general articles will be found under the generic term. To expand a class completely the searcher would have to search under all the specific headings which, taken together, will add up to the broader class.

For example, if we should want to broaden the search on Polyethylene to include all polymers, it would not be sufficient to search under Polymers. It would be necessary to search under the names of all possible polymers. Narrowing a search is achieved in Chemical Abstracts Indexes through the consideration of modifying phrases which are intended to increase the specificity of the index terms.[5]

It is obvious that, compared to a system with no vocabulary control, the system with a controlled vocabulary provides a great deal of guidance to the informed searcher both before and during searching. Clearly defined index characteristics will help in the formulation of search strategies and feedback from the system will assist in the useful modification of the search program. Searching will hold fewer unknowns in the sense that the control of index terms and the display of relationships among them will allow the searcher to have a better feel of what he actually covered or did not cover in his search. It should be remembered, however, that this kind of increased control over the search is only one of many factors influencing overall retrieval effectiveness.

EVALUATION OF RETRIEVAL SYSTEMS

While there has been a great deal of interest in the problems related to the evaluation of the performance of index languages and retrieval systems, there seems to be very little agreement about the basis for evaluation.

One of the major problems in evaluating the performance of retrieval systems has been the lack of purely objective, quantitative measures. While some evaluative criteria are relatively easy to quantify, others do not readily lend themselves to measurement. Examples of relatively easily quantifiable criteria are cost, speed, physical characteristics, response time, and coverage. However, when a system's effectiveness is to be evaluated in terms of its ability to find information relevant to information requests, the concept of relevance is introduced. In the process of determining the relevance of a given document to a given question quantitative measurement becomes difficult.

Cleverdon suggests that all evaluative criteria fall in one of two groups. He calls the first group "user criteria" because it is made up of those factors which are of concern to the users of the system. These are:

1. The ability of a system to present all relevant documents (recall).

2. The ability of the system to withhold no relevant documents (precision, relevance).

3. The interval between the demand being made and the answer being given (response time).

4. The physical form of the output.

5. The effort, intellectual and physical, demanded of the user.

The second group of criteria is related to things with which the user is not directly concerned, which are the concern of the managers of the system. These are such things as the intellectual methods that are adopted to achieve particular results, or the economics of the techniques used. [6]

Among the user criteria listed, the first two, recall and precision, are those which are most difficult to measure, and which are most crucial in any measure of effectiveness. These involve measures around which a considerable amount of research activity as well as controversy have developed.

Evaluative Measures

The two most frequently used measures to evaluate

the performance of document retrieval systems are the re-call ratio and the precision (relevance) ratio. The two ratios measure a system's ability to maximize the number of relevant documents retrieved and to minimize the number of non-relevant documents retrieved in response to a query. They are not intended to measure other system criteria--such as response time, user effort, and economic efficiency--that relate to the overall performance of retrieval systems.

Expressed as a percentage, the recall ratio equals the number of relevant documents retrieved, over the number of known relevant documents in the collection, times 100; and the precision ratio equals the number of relevant documents retrieved, over the total number of documents retrieved in searching, times 100.

The recall ratio means that if, for example, a retrieval system contains ten documents that are relevant to a given question, and in a search six of these are retrieved, then the recall ratio for that particular search is six over ten, times 100, which equals 60%.

This figure is not very meaningful by itself because it is obviously possible to get 100% recall by examining the entire collection. The recall figure in itself is not an exact reflection of the filtering capabilities of the retrieval system. As a filter the retrieval system should reduce the number of documents that need to be looked at while allowing achievement of a satisfactory recall figure. To measure the filtering ability of an indexing system the precision ratio was introduced. Thus, in the previous example, if in order to retrieve six relevant documents we had to retrieve a total of sixty documents, then the precision ratio for this search would be six over sixty, times 100, which equals 10%.

When the two measures are applied together they should indicate what proportion of the total number of relevant documents in the collection has been retrieved and at what cost (in terms of noise) a particular performance is achieved.[6]

Some difficulties related to the application of these measures should be pointed out. The use of the recall ratio for evaluation requires knowledge of every relevant document in the collection for a given query and this becomes impossible to ascertain in a large operational situation.

Relevance Experimentation

The concept of relevance is implicit in the evaluative measures just discussed and is of considerable interest to information scientists. Relevance has been the subject of many debates, yet there is little agreement about such things as the nature of relevance, how relevance should be described and measured, who should judge it and from what point of view. A great deal of research and experimentation during the last decade has been concerned with the problem of relevance, particularly with the effects of a variety of variables on human relevance judgments.

The major classes of variables that have been investigated are: documents and document representations, queries, judgmental situations, modes of expression, and human characteristics.

The document has been found to be an important variable influencing relevance judgments. Such things as the style of the document and the specificity of its subject content, as compared to the subject content of the query, are found to be significant characteristics. Relevance judgments are also found to differ depending upon the form of the document, and whether the judgment was based on full text, title, or an abstract.

Some of the more interesting findings relating to the effect of the query on relevance judgments are that a close correlation exists between texts of queries and texts of relevant documents; that the more the judges know about the query the higher is the agreement among them on relevance and the more stringent the judgments become; and, that the less one knows about the query the greater the tendency to judge documents relevant.

Studies concerned with the effect of time and stringency measures on judgmental situations have found that high pressure tends to stimulate the rating of documents as relevant.

The ways in which the judgment is to be expressed--scales, ratings, etc.--also influence the outcome of relevance judgments. For example, different scales may produce slightly different judgments and the end points of scales tend to be used most heavily.

A fundamental factor studied in all experiments was the effect on relevance judgments of some human characteristics, particularly those related to subject or professional education. Subject knowledge seems to be the most important human characteristic affecting relevance judgments, and the level of the judge's subject knowledge varies inversely with the number of documents judged relevant. It was also found that judging relevance is not the same as judging non-relevance, and that it is easier to get agreement on what is not relevant than on what is relevant.[7]

The Cranfield Experiments

In the first Aslib-Cranfield experiment evaluative measures were used to test the comparative efficiency of four different indexing systems: an alphabetical subject catalog, the Universal Decimal Classification, a faceted classification, and the Uniterm system of coordinate indexing. In terms of performance it was found that all four systems operated at about the same level of efficiency.[8]

The first Cranfield experiment tried to overcome the problems related to judging relevancy by basing each test question on a document in the collection, which was called a source document in relation to that question. Then, the basic test was simply this: for a given system, in an average search for a hundred questions, how many of the equivalent source documents would be found? This figure was the recall ratio and was found to be between 75 and 85 percent for all systems tested. It was also found that most (60%) of the failures were due to inadequacies or inaccuracies in the indexing process rather than to faults of the indexing system.

In the next stage of the experiment the two ratios were used to compare the efficiency of the Western Reserve University's Index to Metallurgical Literature with that of a manual faceted catalog, and a somewhat more sophisticated experimental method was employed. A question document matrix was derived which indicated for each document, in relation to each question, whether it was a source document, equal in relevance to a source document, of minor relevance, or irrelevant. When the figures for both recall and precision were combined it was found that an inverse relationship existed between them, and that once an optimum level of performance had been reached, any device added to a system to improve recall must reduce precision; conversely, any device added to a system to improve precision must reduce recall. Evidence suggested that roughly, within the normal operating range of a system, a 1% improvement in precision will cost a 3% drop in recall.

At the same time, the effect of specificity and exhaustivity on the performance of retrieval systems was also tested. It was found that specificity of index language makes for higher precision and lower recall, and that higher exhaustivity in indexing produces higher recall and low precision. It was also reported by Cleverdon that "the test of the Western Reserve University Index appeared to indicate that there was an optimum level of exhaustivity of indexing, for a higher level of exhaustivity did not significantly improve recall but it weakened precision, while a low level of exhaustivity inhibited maximum recall." [9]

The first Cranfield experiment concerning the comparative efficiency of retrieval systems generated considerable discussion and controversy. A major part of the criticism centered around the experimental design and the methodology used. Swanson questioned such things as the source document concept, the close correlation between questions and titles, titles and indexing, and the role of human memory, because some of the same people did the searching who did the indexing.[10] Taube argued about the concept of relevance, in his article on what he called the "pseudo-mathematics of relevance."[11] Rees expressed doubt about the existence of a fixed relevance for a document to an information requirement for all users at all times.[12]

In the second Cranfield project variations of five main indexing languages, a total of thirty-three different indexing methods, were investigated. The relevance of every question to every document in the collection was determined by the originators of the questions and a relevance scale of 1 to 4 was used in the following way:

1. References which are a complete answer to the question.

2. References of high degree of relevance, the lack of which either would have made the research impracticable or would have resulted in a considerable amount of extra work.

3. References which were useful, either as general background to the work or as suggesting methods of tack-

ling certain aspects of the work.

4. References of minimum interest, for example those that have been included from a historical viewpoint.

A recent study raises some questions relating to the experimental design used in Cranfield II and strongly suggests that the relevance assessments made are faulty in the sense that many relevant documents were not so identified by the judges. It is also pointed out that the ranking of indexing methods may change if the missed relevant documents are taken into consideration. [13, 14]

The MEDLARS Evaluation Study

The recent MEDLARS evaluation[15] is an extensive study concerned with the evaluation of the operating efficiency of a large on-going computer based document retrieval system. A detailed description of both the MEDLARS system and the evaluation study is given in the unit on Representative Machine Applications.

Cost-Effectiveness of Retrieval Systems

Consideration of cost versus effectiveness, until fairly recently, has been of relatively little interest to designers of retrieval systems. Admittedly, on the basis of the problems involved in measurements of performance and the difficulty in quantifying the intangible benefits of retrieval systems, effectiveness is not easy to determine. Nevertheless, too little emphasis has frequently been placed on such reasonably attainable goals as sound systems design and rigorous cost control.

Cost-effectiveness is concerned with the relationship between level of performance (effectiveness) and the cost of achieving this level. Cost-benefit refers to the relationship between the benefits of a particular product or service and the cost of providing it. Because cost, performance, and benefits are closely interrelated within the environment of a retrieval system, the relationships between cost and effectiveness and cost and benefit are frequently difficult to distinguish.

Cost-effectiveness analysis of a retrieval system involves the study of tradeoffs, break-even points, and diminishing returns relating to such factors as system coverage, indexing policies and procedures, searching procedures, and modes of interaction between system and user. The objective of the analysis is to determine the most efficient combination of procedures in terms of cost for obtaining a particular level of performance.

The performance of a retrieval system can be measured in terms of recall power, precision power, coverage, response time, and the amount of time and effort required from the user. Possible criteria for measuring the benefits of a retrieval system are:

1) Cost savings resulting from finding information via this particular system versus obtaining it from elsewhere.

2) Avoidance of loss of productivity that would result if information from the system were not available.

3) Improved decision making due to the availability of information.

4) Avoidance of duplication of work that has been worked on before by other researchers.

5) Stimulation of thinking and invention.[16]

References

1. Meadow, Charles T. The Analysis of Information Systems. New York, Wiley, 1967. (Chapter 6. The Organization of Files.)

2. Warheit, I. A. "File Organization of Library Records," Journal of Library Automation, 2:20-30, March 1969.

3. Fairthorne, Robert A. Toward Information Retrieval. London, Butterworths, 1961. p. 136.

4. Artandi, Susan. "Document Description and Representation." In: Annual Review of Information Science and Technology, Vol. 5. Chicago, Encyclopaedia Britannica, 1970. pp. 143-167.

5. Artandi, Susan. "The Searchers--Links Between Inquirers and Indexes," Special Libraries, 57:571-574, October 1966.

6. Cleverdon, Cyril W., Jack Mills and Michael Keen. Factors Determining the Performance of Indexing Systems. Vol. 1. Design. Cranfield, 1966.

7. Saracevic, Tefko. "Ten Years of Relevance Experimentation--A Summary and Synthesis of Conclusions." In: Proceedings of the American Society for Information Science, Vol. 7. 1970. pp. 33-36.

8. Cleverdon, Cyril W. Report on the Testing and Analysis of an Investigation into the Comparative Efficiency of Indexing Systems. Cranfield, 1962.

9. Cleverdon, Cyril W., Frederick W. Lancaster, and Jack Mills. "Uncovering Some Facts of Life in Information Retrieval," Special Libraries, 55:86-91, February 1964.

10. Swanson, Don R. "The Evidence Underlying the Cranfield Results," Library Quarterly, 35:1-20, January 1965.

11. Taube, Mortimer. "A Note on the Pseudo-Mathematics of Relevance," American Documentation, 16:62-72, April 1965. Subsequent exchange of letters, 16:341, October 1965.

12. Rees, Alan M. "The Relevance of Relevance to the Testing and Evaluation of Document Retrieval Systems," Aslib Proceedings, 18:316-323, November 1966.

13. Swanson, Don R. "Some Unexplained Aspects of the Cranfield Tests of Indexing Performance Factors," Library Quarterly, 41:223-228, July 1971.

14. Harter, Stephen P. "The Cranfield II Relevance Assessments: A Critical Evaluation," Library Quarterly, 41:229-235, July 1971.

15. Lancaster, Frederick W. "MEDLARS: Report on the Evaluation of Its Operating Efficiency," American Documentation, 20:119-142, April 1969.

16. Lancaster, Frederick W. "Cost-Effectiveness Analysis of Information Retrieval and Dissemination Systems," Journal of the American Society for Information Science, 22:12-27, January-February 1971.

PART III

COMPUTER BASED SYSTEMS

CHAPTER 5

COMPUTER HARDWARE
AND SOFTWARE

> The Digital Computer
>
> Data Representation for
> Computer Processing
>
> Programming Languages
>
> Computer Time-Sharing

THE DIGITAL COMPUTER

Document retrieval applications have been utilizing the digital computer as distinguished from the analog computer. The digital computer operates on data represented by discrete sets of digits. In contrast, the analog computer operates on data represented in continuous form in terms of some measurable physical quality that varies in proportion to the actual data it represents. The analog and digital machines have evolved from the concepts of measuring and counting, respectively.

Analog information is generated on quantities such as voltage, temperature, velocity, and pressure through the transformation of information from one physical form to another. For example, the thermometer transforms temperature information into the position information of a mercury column. Other familiar examples of analog devices are speedometers, bathroom scales, and barometers.

In contrast with analog information, digital information is discrete information and is characterized by the fact that it may be coded by the use of symbols or combination of symbols. Figure 6 shows the same set of data expressed in analog and digital form. In one case the values of x and y are expressed by an analog of length. In the other case the values of x and y are given as numbers (expressed in numerical symbols).

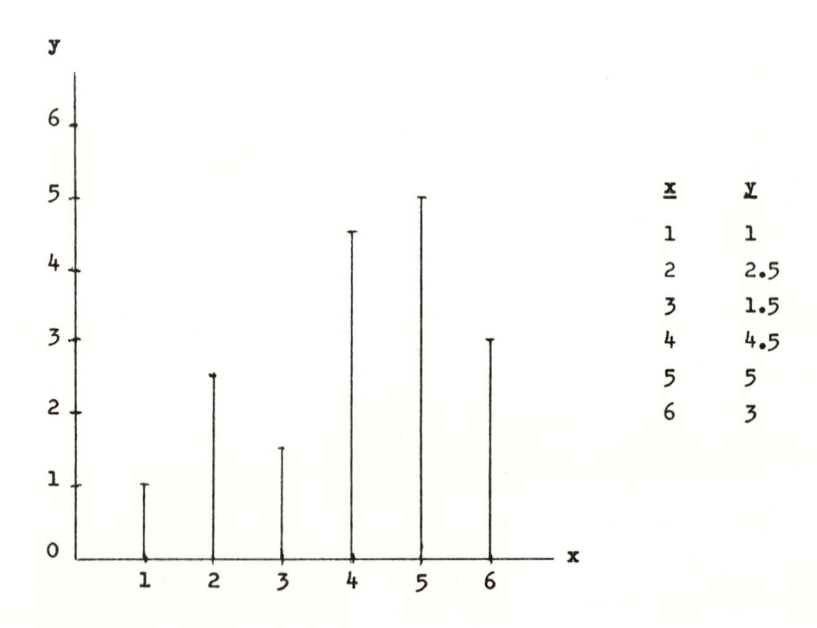

x	y
1	1
2	2.5
3	1.5
4	4.5
5	5
6	3

Figure 6.   Information in Analog and Digital Form

The digital computer's basic characteristic is that it can distinguish between two physical states such as the direction of magnetization of a ferrite core, or whether voltage is present or absent. It functions in what is called a binary mode, which means that computer components can indicate only two possible states or conditions. Data are represented in the computer through these binary indications by assigning specific values to them.

While the ancestry of the computer can be traced to Charles Babbage's Analytical Engine of 1834, the first true computer, Mark I, was built in the early 1940's by Howard Aiken at Harvard.

Computer Hardware and Software 89

A major step toward modern computers came from the recognition of compatibility between symbolic logic and electrical network theory. In 1938 Claude Shannon expressed this relationship in his famous paper, "A Symbolic Analysis of Relay and Switching Circuits," published in the Transactions of the American Institute of Electrical Engineers.[1] The paper explained the basis for logical computer design and showed how to instruct computers to perform logical as well as arithmetic operations.

Early computers, referred to as first generation machines, used vacuum tubes in their circuits. They were relatively expensive, unreliable, and bulky. In the late 1950's these machines were superseded by transistorized second generation computers. Third generation computers use microcircuits. Microcircuitry increases reliability and speed and, at the same time, results in reduction in bulk.

Some computers are designed for specific problems; these are called special purpose computers. Digital computers that can be programmed to solve a variety of problems are called general purpose computers. In a modern digital computer the program, a sequence of machine instructions arranged to accomplish a given task, is stored in the computer in the same form as the data. This is why it is referred to as an internally programmed or stored-program machine.

Associated with each computer is the operating system, a machine-dependent super-program that controls the overall performance of the machine. The operating system is stored in memory and its complexity and size usually increase with the sophistication of the capabilities of a particular machine.

The programming system required for a data processing operation is called software, in contrast with the hardware of the computer system itself.

All digital computers have five major elements: Input, Control, Logical/Arithmetic, Storage (memory), and Output. The organization of these components to form a computer may be illustrated as in Figure 7.

```
                    ┌──────────┐
                    │ STORAGE  │
                    │ (MEMORY) │
                    └────┬─────┘
                         ↕
Data      ┌───────┐  ┌────────┐      ┌────────┐
──────→   │ INPUT │→ │CONTROL │ ───→ │ OUTPUT │ ──→
PROGRAM   └───────┘  └────┬───┘      └────────┘
                          ↕
                    ┌──────────┐
                    │ LOGICAL/ │
                    │ARITHMETIC│
                    └──────────┘
```

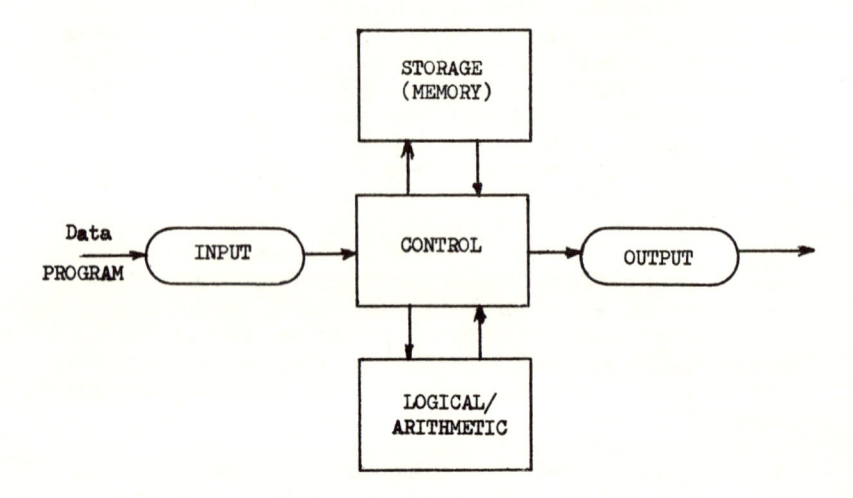

Figure 7. The Organization of the Digital Computer

In the execution of a program the computer performs the following sequence of operations:

The program and the data to be used are entered into storage through the input device. Entering the program and the data into storage is done under the supervision of the control unit. Next, under the supervision of the control unit, the logical/arithmetic unit performs the following operations:

1) Obtains data from storage;

2) Operates on the data as prescribed by the program;

3) Returns the results to storage.

Finally, under the instruction of the program, the results are transferred to the output unit.

The Binary Concept

Data are represented within the computer by assign-

Computer Hardware and Software 91

ing a specific value to a binary indication or to groups of binary indications.

Binary codes are made up of two symbols, zero and one, corresponding to the two-state nature of the devices used. The actual forms of the two symbols vary; it may be the presence or absence of a hole in paper tape, the direction of magnetization of a spot on magnetic tape, or the magnetic polarization of a core in one or the other direction. The binary notations 0 and 1 are commonly used to designate _bits_, and alphabetic and numeric (alphanumeric) characters are expressed in terms of bits. The number of bits needed per character will depend on the number of unique character codes that need to be represented. This can be calculated mathematically as follows:

The number of possible codes = 2^n

where 2 is the number of different symbols available in the binary code and $\underline{n}$ is the number of positions or bits per character.

Using 6 bits per character will allow representation of 2^6 = 64 different codes or alphanumeric characters; 5 bits per character would give only 2^5 = 32 different characters.

This relationship between the number of possible unique code representations and the number of bits per character is particularly significant in text processing, where the number of different characters to be represented may run into the hundreds. The increase in the number of bits per character will result in a reduction of the amount of information that can be stored in a computer memory of a given storage capacity.

In some computers the values associated with the binary notation are directly related to the binary number system. Similar to the decimal system, the binary system is a positional number system, in which the value of each digit in the number is determined by the digit, the position of the digit in the number, and the base or radix of the number system. The base is defined as the number of different digits which can occur in a given position in the number. The decimal system is a base 10 system because there are ten basic digits (0, 1, 2, 3, 4, 5, 6, 7, 8, 9) from which the number system is formulated. The value of each digit depends on its position in the number. For example, in the three decimal numbers 650, 560, 456, the digit 6 signifies respectively 6 x 100, 6 x 10, and 6 x 1.

The binary number system is a base 2 system in which there are two basic digits 0 and 1. The positional value of the symbols 0 and 1 is based on the progression of powers of 2. The unit position has a value of 1, the next position a value of 2, the next 4, the next 8, and so on.

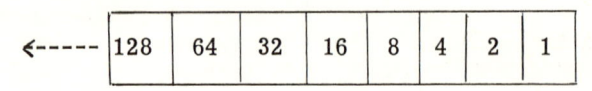

<-----	128	64	32	16	8	4	2	1

Figure 8. Place Value of Binary Numbers

Binary Representations of Decimal Numbers

In pure binary notation the 1 bit represents the presence of a value and the 0 bit represents its absence. The following shows decimal numbers and their corresponding binary representations.

Decimal value	Binary representation
	16 8 4 2 1 place values
0	0 0 0 0 0
1	0 0 0 0 1
2	0 0 0 1 0
3	0 0 0 1 1
4	0 0 1 0 0
5	0 0 1 0 1
6	0 0 1 1 0
7	0 0 1 1 1
8	0 1 0 0 0
9	0 1 0 0 1

Computer Hardware and Software 93

```
Decimal value          Binary representation
                       16  8  4  2  1   place values
     .                         .
     .                         .
     .                         .
     16                 1  0  0  0  0
     24                 1  1  0  0  0
```

Figure 9. Decimal Numbers and Their Corresponding Binary Representations

DATA REPRESENTATION FOR COMPUTER PROCESSING

To process information by computer it must be represented in a form that is acceptable to the computer and can be recognized by it. Since the basic characteristic of the digital computer is that it can distinguish between two identifiable physical states, information must be transformed into binary form to be computer processed. In other words, the various methods of data representation for computer processing are based on the binary nature of digital computers.

In computer processing we are concerned with three types of data representation:

1) Representation for input to the computer;

2) Output representation;

3) Representation for storage.

A general problem related to data representation for input and output has been the fact that while internal processing has become faster and less expensive, input/output devices have not kept pace with the increases in the speed and cost/effectiveness of main frames. Computers have improved their cost/effectiveness by factors of more than 1000 since the first Univac I was delivered in 1951; input/output devices, however, have improved by much smaller factors. The reasons are quite obvious. While computers operate in the nanosecond (one-billionth of a second) time range, input/output devices must frequently interface with humans who operate in the minutes to seconds time frame. This is especially true of keyboarding operations where cost/effectiveness is further affected by the steady increase in labor costs and a steady decrease in the cost of computer time.

Data Representation for Input

Data conversion for input to the computer can be accomplished in several ways, such as keyboarding, automatic character recognition, voice recognition, and through "writing" on a cathode ray tube or some other device. In all cases the device used will convert information from some other form to binary form.

Keyboarding

The most commonly used methods of conversion for machine input involve some kind of keyboarding operation. Keyboarding may result in recording information on punched cards, punched paper tape, magnetic tape, magnetic disk, or it may mean direct entry into the computer through a typewriter, a remote teletype terminal, or a Touch-Tone (R) telephone (See also section on terminals). In all keyboarding methods speed of recording or speed of input in case of direct input is limited by the speed of the human operator.

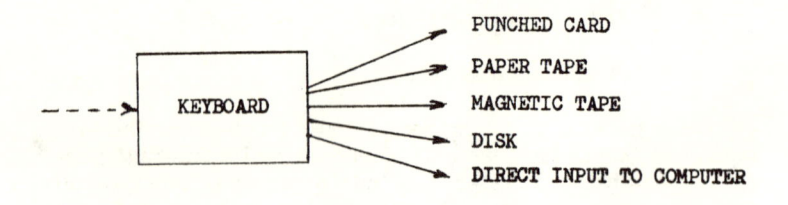

```
                              ──► PUNCHED CARD
                              ──► PAPER TAPE
   ─ ─ ─► │ KEYBOARD │ ────── ──► MAGNETIC TAPE
                              ──► DISK
                              ──► DIRECT INPUT TO COMPUTER
```

Figure 10.

Punched Cards

Data are recorded on a punched card by means of a keypunch. The keypunch has a keyboard similar to that of a typewriter. Data being punched may simultaneously be printed on the top edge of the card, depending on the type of punch used. The keypunch operates serially, one column at a time.

The presence or absence of holes on a punched card is sensed by the card reader and is converted into electrical impulses to be transmitted to the computer. The most frequently used punched card, the IBM punched card, has 80 vertical columns with twelve punching positions in each column. One or more punches on a single column are used to represent a numeric, alphabetic, or special character. Thus the maximum number of characters that can be represented on a single IBM card is 80.

The twelve punching positions are divided into two areas. The first ten punching positions from the bottom edge of the card are numbered and have a value of 0-9. The remaining two positions are not numbered and are referred to as 11 and 12. Numeric characters are represented by a single punch in a vertical column. The alphabetic characters A through I are represented by a 12 punch and a numeric punch, 1 through 9, respectively. The alphabetic characters J through R use the 11 punch and a numeric punch 1 through 9, respectively. S through Z use the 0 punch and a numeric punch 2 through 9, respectively. Special characters are represented by one, two, or three punches in a single column and consist of punch configurations not used to represent alphabetic or numeric characters.

Paper Tape

Data on paper tape are represented through the arrangement of punched holes along the length of the tape. Paper tape is a continuous medium and is not limited to the fixed number of characters that can be represented on a single punched card. A number of different kinds of paper tape and character codes for recording information on them are currently in use. One example is the eight channel tape which has eight parallel channels along the length of

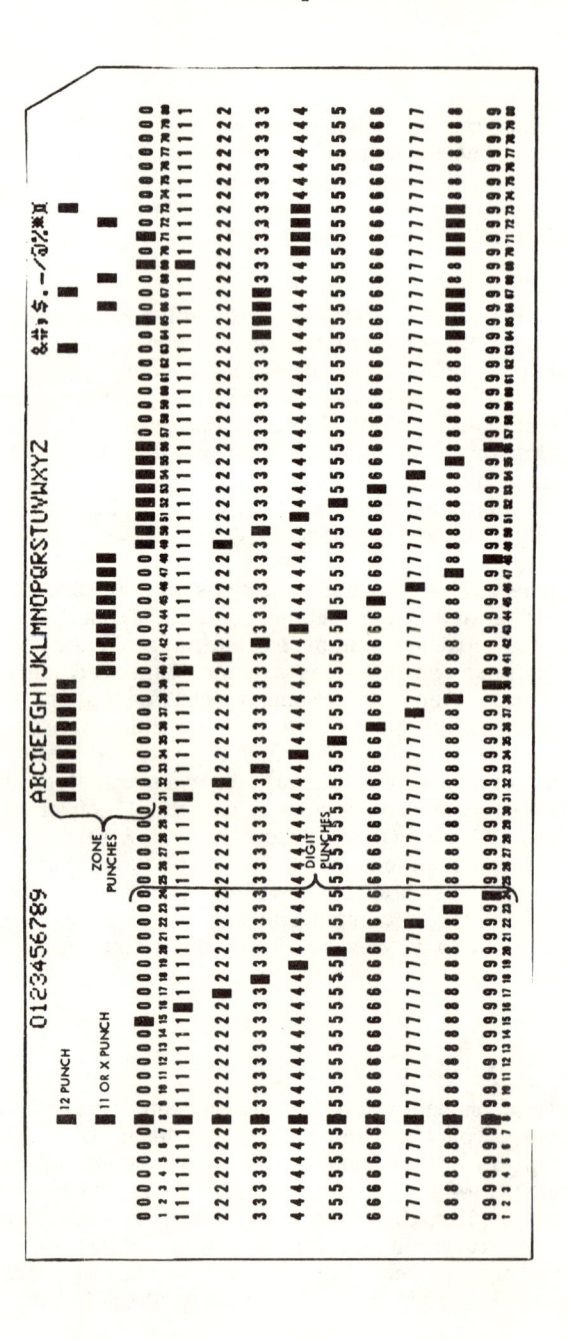

Figure 11. IBM Punched Card

the tape. One column across the width of the tape (in this case eight possible punching positions) represents one character. The lower four channels of the tape are used to record numeric characters and have the values 1, 2, 4, and 8. Numeric values 0 through 9 can be represented through a punch or a combination of punches in these four positions. For example, a hole in channel 2 represents a numeric 2; a combination of punches in 1, 2, and 4 represent a numeric 7. The second and third channels from the top, X and 0 are used in combination with the numeric channels to represent alphabetic and special characters. For example, a combination of punches in X, 0, and 1 represents the letter A. A punch in the topmost EL channel indicates the end of a record.

A check hole is used as part of the checking system to ensure that each character is recorded correctly. A commonly used method is the odd-parity check which requires that each column of the tape must be punched with an odd number of holes. This means that a check hole must be present in any column whose basic code consists of an even number of holes. A variety of automatic tape producing typewriters are available. They produce hard copy simultaneously with paper tape which can be used for checking the accuracy of the keyboarding operation.[2]

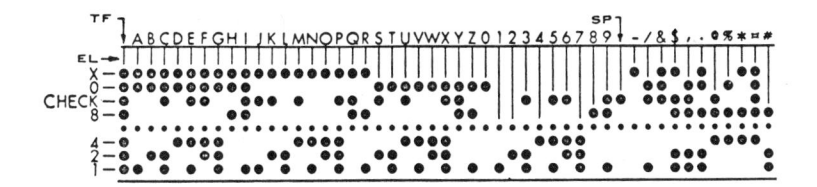

Figure 12. Paper Tape, Eight-Channel Code

Magnetic Tape

Magnetic tape has two principal uses in computer processing. It is used as input/output device and as an external storage device. The amount of information that can be stored in the main storage area of the computer is limited. When large quantities of data need to be processed it becomes necessary to use some form of external storage. Magnetic tape is frequently used for this purpose. Other types of external storage devices will be discussed later.

Two forms of keyboard-to-magnetic tape devices have been developed recently for data conversion for input. One is a device that will record the keyed-in information electronically on computer-compatible magnetic tape and allow the operator to enter the information that was captured on the tape automatically into the computer. The second type of device uses a typewriter keyboard for the recording of data on non-computer-compatible magnetic tape in cartridges, or cassettes. The cassette or cartridge devices are similar to the keyboard-to-tape units, with the cartridge or cassette being an intermediate between the keyboard and the computer-compatible input. They have found increasing use in the handling of textual data not normally or economically handled on keypunch equipment. [3]

As an input/output medium magnetic tape is desirable because of its reliability and high rate of data transmission. In large computing systems, reading information from cards or paper tape is very much slower than the internal processing of information. For this reason it is very common to transfer information from punched cards or paper tape to magnetic tape prior to input.

Magnetic tape is quite similar to paper tape except that, instead of holes, data are represented through the arrangement of magnetized spots along the length of the tape, in rows called tracks. A read/write head accomplishes the sensing and writing of information on the tape. Depending on the equipment used, tape may be moving at high speed or may be motionless during writing. A character is represented by small magnetized sections of the channels located vertically across the width of the tape. The recording on tape can be retained indefinitely or the tape can be re-used many times. It should be noted, however, that when new information is "written" on tape it will automatically replace any information that was previously recorded on it. The tape is a 1/2-inch wide plastic ribbon coated with a magnetic oxide material. It comes on a 10-1/2-inch diameter reel holding either 1,200 or 2,400 feet of tape. How much information can be stored on a given length of tape depends on the recording density used, which in turn is determined by the closeness of the columns of magnetized sections across the width of the tape. Placing them close together is called packing the tape. Most magnetic tape units provide the user with an option of recording information at high or low density.

On a seven-track magnetic tape each character is recorded in a seven-bit code consisting of zeros and ones with a checking requirement of an even number of ones. Records on tape can be of any length, and are separated from each other by a 3/4-inch piece of blank tape called the <u>interrecord gap</u>, or interblock gap when records are blocked.

Some important tape characteristics are the following:

<u>Density:</u> the number of characters that can be recorded on a linear inch of tape. Expressed in characters or bits per inch.

<u>Tape speed:</u> the speed of the tape as it passes the read/write head. Expressed in inches per second.

<u>Character time:</u> the time required to read or write one character. Expressed in milliseconds.

<u>Character rate:</u> the maximum rate of reading or writing characters. Expressed in characters per second. It is determined by the combination of tape speed and density rate.

<u>Effective character rate:</u> determined by multiplying the number of characters per record by the number of records and dividing this product by the read/write time in seconds for the tape speed used. It is expressed in characters per second. Read/write time takes into consideration not only the time required to read and write a tape record but also the time needed to accelerate the tape to full speed after a stop when the previous record was completed.

<u>Access time:</u> the time required to reach a tape record from the immediately preceding one. Includes time to space over interrecord gap. Expressed in milliseconds.

<u>Rewind time:</u> the time required to rewind a reel of tape. Expressed in minutes.

The relationships among these tape characteristics

100   Computers in Information Science

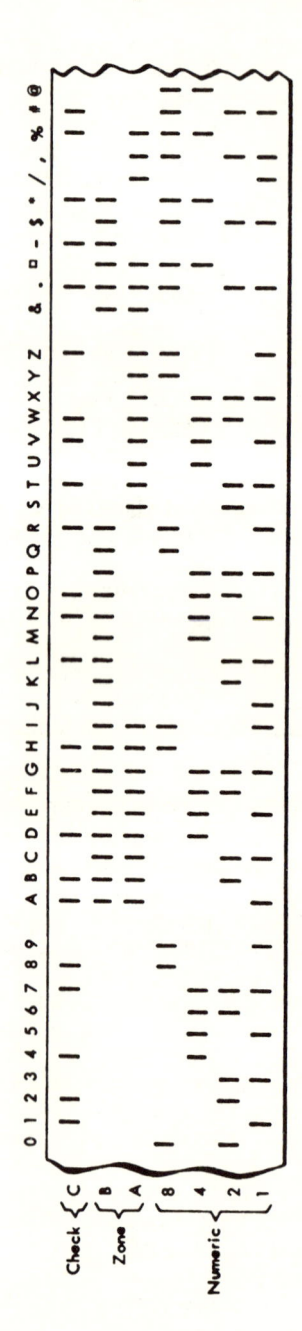

Figure 13. Magnetic Tape, Seven-Track, Seven-Bit Alphameric Code

Computer Hardware and Software 101

Characters per Record	Read Time (Seconds), 100 Records		Characters per Record	Effective Character Rate		
	200 CPI	556 CPI		200 CPI	556 CPI	
360	7.08	3.88	360	5,084	9,278	
720	12.08	5.68	720	5,960	12,676	
1,800	27.10	11.08	1,800	6,642	16,245	
3,600	51.04	20.08	3,600	7,053	17,928	

Tape Speed: 36 Inches per Second

Characters per Record	Read Time (Seconds), 100 Records			Characters per Record	Effective Character Rate		
	200 CPI	556 CPI	800 CPI		200 CPI	556 CPI	800 CPI
360	3.49	1.94	1.69	360	10,315	18,556	21,301
720	5.90	2.81	2.30	720	12,203	25,623	31,304
1,800	13.40	5.40	4.14	1,800	13,699	33,333	43,478
3,600	25.20	9.72	7.20	3,600	14,286	37,037	50,000

Tape Speed: 75 Inches per Second

Characters per Record	Read Time (Seconds), 100 Records				Characters per Record	Effective Character Rate			
	200 CPI	556 CPI	800 CPI	1,511 CPI		200 CPI	556 CPI	800 CPI	1,511 CPI
360	2.31	1.30	1.12	0.63	360	15,584	27,692	32,142	57,142
720	3.90	1.88	1.52	1.85	720	18,461	38,298	47,368	84,705
1,800	8.65	3.61	2.71	1.5	1,800	20,809	49,861	66,420	120,000
3,600	16.57	6.49	4.69	2.6	3,600	21,726	55,470	76,759	138,461

Tape Speed: 112.5 In. per Second

Figure 14. Reading Times and Effective Character Rates for Magnetic Tape Records

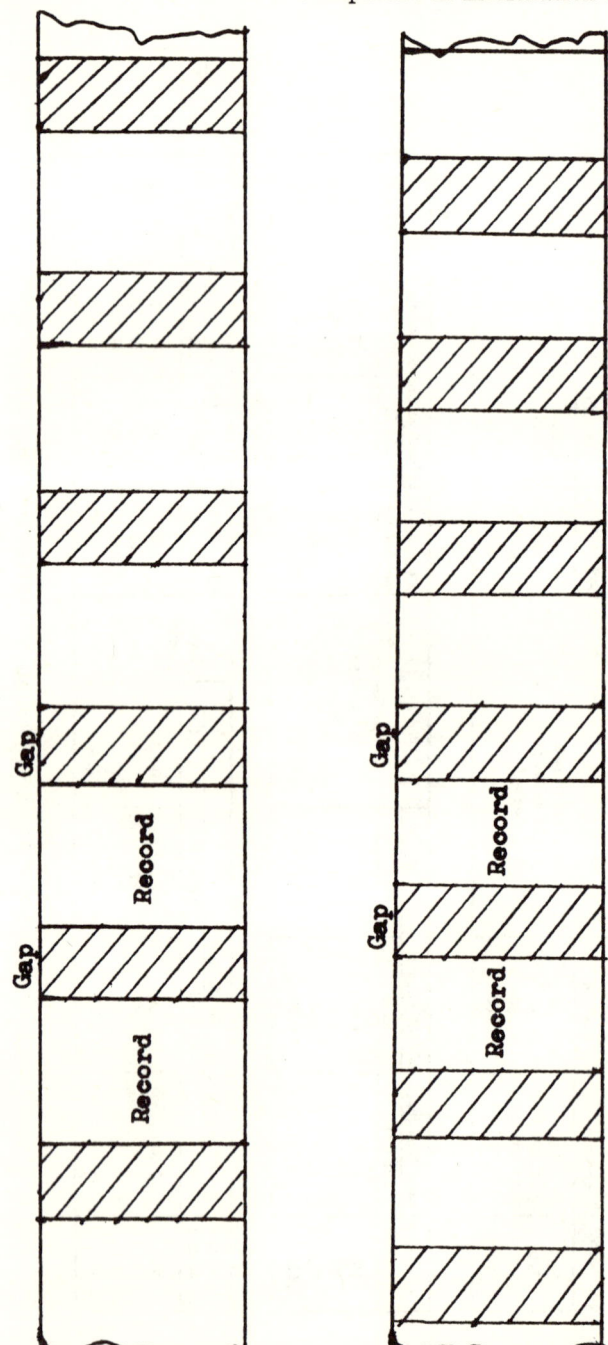

Fig. 15. Arrangement of Records on Magnetic Tape

Computer Hardware and Software

are easy to see. The average length of the record will determine how much of the tape will be utilized for storage of information. For example, if the average length is 3/4-inch, only half of the tape will be utilized. The length of the record (or the number of records on a given length of tape) will affect effective character rate. The latter is particularly important in the type of computer processing in which large amounts of alphabetic information are involved, as is the case in document retrieval.

The following examples illustrate the effect of record length and recording density on effective character rate.

Example 1

100 records
720 characters/record
200 characters/inch
tape speed = 36 inches/second

Effective character rate:

100 x 720 = 72,000

Read time in seconds for 720 characters per record at 36 inches/sec. is 12.08 seconds

$\frac{72,000}{12.08}$ = 5,960 char/sec

Example 2

100 records
360 characters/record
200 characters/inch
tape speed = 36 inches/second

Effective character rate:

100 x 360 = 36,000

Read time in seconds for 360 characters per record at 36 inches/sec. is 7.08 seconds

$\frac{36,000}{7.08}$ = 5,084 char/sec

Effective character rate goes up with the increase in number of characters per record.

Optical Character Recognition

Optical character recognition has great potential usefulness for information retrieval applications because it could alleviate the bottlenecks resulting from the need to convert large amounts of alpha-numeric information into machine readable form. In contrast with the usual keyboarding operation, optical character readers read printed text and introduce the data into the computer system automatically. The key element of the optical character reader is an optical scanner consisting of a powerful light source and a lens system that can distinguish variations in the intensity of light reflected from the printed page. The light patterns which result through scanning are converted into electrical impulses to develop a character pattern. When the optically read character pattern matches the character pattern in the reader's recognition circuits, the character is recorded and transferred into the computer system for processing.

Some of the readers which have been developed can recognize only special fonts. Others are able to read a number of commercially used fonts but are extremely expensive, which means that the keyboarding volume must be quite high before their use becomes economical.

Because of multiple-font and cost problems, the application of optical character recognition in information retrieval is currently rather limited. Greater flexibility and reliability in the recognition of type fonts is needed before optical character recognition can be used for large scale input of materials from the published literature. [4]

Computer input microfilm (CIM) refers to various methods of scanning microfilm to convert it into digital form for computer input.

Voice Recognition

Devices that can recognize human speech have been developed on an experimental basis; however, they are capable of handling only very limited vocabularies in the 30- to 100-word range. Progress in the development of these devices has been slow because of the tremendous technical problems involved. Voice recognition devices must be able to handle such things as variations in speech intensity levels, detect the onset time of each word through proper segmentation of words in a sentence, differentiate between the voice of a speaker and background noise, and recognize the voice message regardless of who the speaker is.

Two basic approaches to voice recognition are direct sampling of voice input and sampling of preprocessed voice input.

Direct sampling of voice input is based on the changes in voltage generated by the microphone and requires a considerable amount of computer processing and storage. The system developed at Stanford University, for example, requires, for each second of voice input, the storage and processing of 180,000 bits.

Preprocessing simplifies voice recognition by reducing the amount of redundancy inherent in voice input signals and can considerably reduce the amount of computer storage and processing required by the direct sampling method.[5]

Graphic Input

Information may be entered into the computer through a cathode ray tube using a light pen. The light pen contains a sensing apparatus that is triggered whenever it is held close to the tube face and senses the spot of displayed light under itself. When the spot is sensed, the pen sends signals to the computer by identifying the x,y coordinates of the point where light was sensed. In order to interpret this message the computer must know what was displayed at any given spot and what it means when the light pen selects that spot.

The computer can be programmed to make selections of displayed alternatives, or to change the position or content of the displayed information. The latter is useful in text editing, for example, when it is necessary to move a word to a different position in a sentence or to change words or add new words. It is also possible to draw a figure with the light pen and the computer will store this information by recording in digital form the locations of the sequence of light dots that correspond to the drawing.

The RAND Tablet is another device for the input of graphic images to a computer. It consists of an array of 1024 x 1024 grid elements embedded in a flat surface. Instead of a light pen, the user writes with a pen-like device that is pressure sensitive. As the pen moves across the surface of the tablet, the positions of the grid intersections that it passes over are made known to the computer and the path of the pen is also displayed on the cathode ray tube that is used in conjunction with the tablet.[6]

Output Representation

A number of output devices record information in binary form on punched cards, on punched paper tape or on magnetic tape. Printers and typewriters provide a permanent visual record of the output of the computer. Output information can also be recorded on microfilm, on a cathode ray tube, or in voice form.

Printers

Printers provide permanent visual records of the output of the computer. Speeds of printing vary from 10 to 2400 characters per second. Printing is achieved when data in electronic form are used to activate printing elements. The major types of printers are the wheel printer, the chain printer, the wire matrix printer, and the console typewriter.

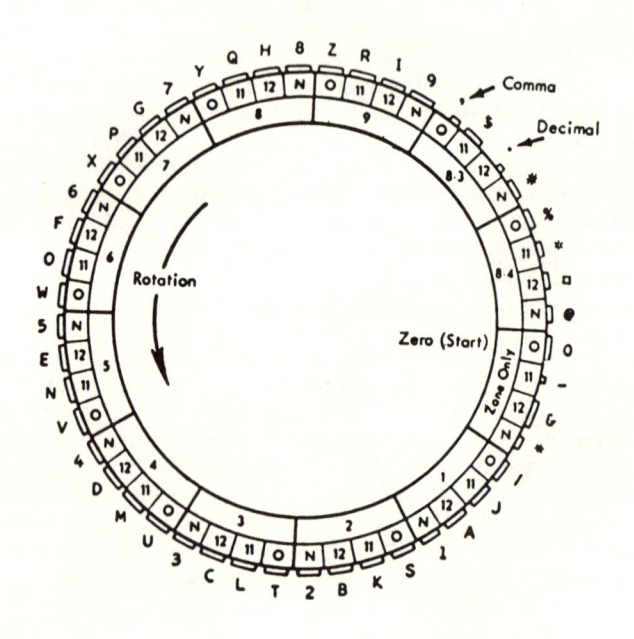

Figure 16. Print Wheel

Computer Hardware and Software

The print wheel printer consists of 120 rotary print wheels, each of which has 48 type characters. The printer prints a complete line of 120 characters at a time by placing the 120 print wheels in the appropriate position.

In the chain printer characters are assembled on a chain. As the chain moves horizontally, each character is printed as it is positioned opposite a magnetically activated hammer that presses the paper against one piece of type on the moving chain. Chains are available with upper and lower case characters and they can be changed easily to provide a choice of print fonts.

In the handling of bibliographic information or in text processing a frequent problem related to printers is caused by the large size of the character set that is needed, and special print trains have been developed to handle this type of processing. For example, to facilitate the printing of the contents of the MARC record (see section on MARC) the Information Systems Office of the Library of Congress developed a print train character set for printing information in all the major Roman alphabet languages and in the romanized form of non-Roman alphabet languages.

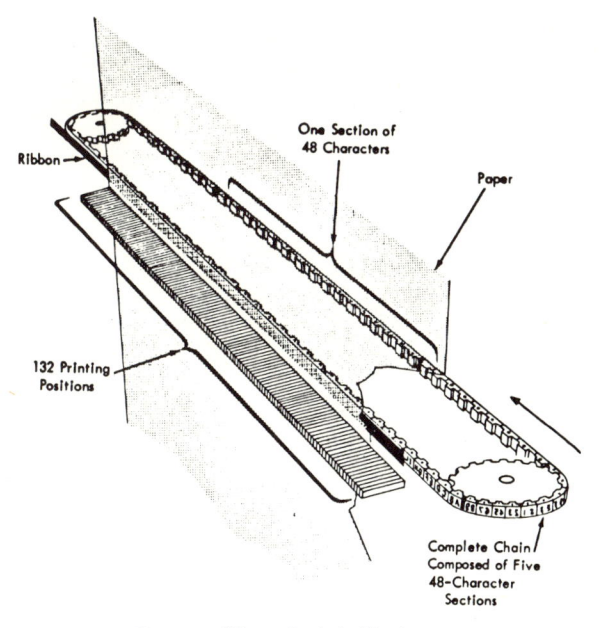

Figure 17. Print Chain

ABCDEFGH
IJKLMNOP
QRSTUVWX
YZ012345
6789-.:&
/◇$+#%@=
(+)

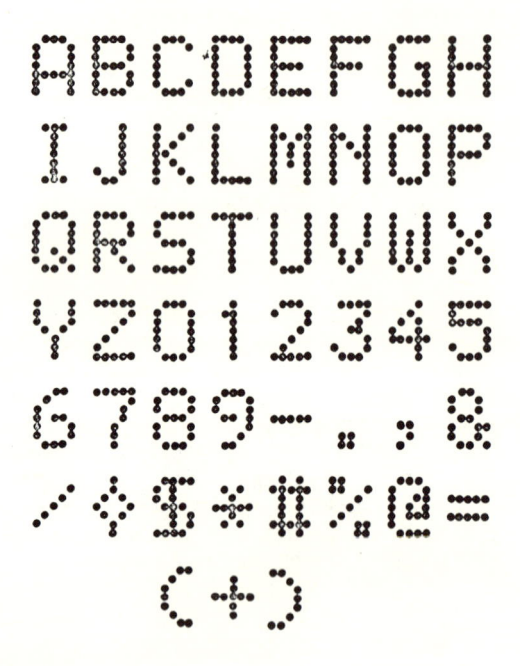

Figure 18. Wire Printing Dot Patterns

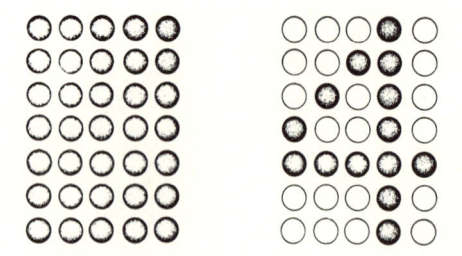

Figure 19. 5 x 7 Dot Pattern

In the wire matrix printer each character is printed as a pattern of dots formed by the ends of small wires arranged in a five-by-seven rectangle. A line of print consists of 120 characters and can be printed at a rate of 500 or 1000 lines per minute, depending on the particular model.[2]

Typewriters are relatively slow output devices and are not used for large scale printing; however, they are frequently used as terminals in interactive computer systems. Both typewriter terminals and video type output devices are discussed in greater detail in the section on computer timesharing.

Computer Composition

In computer composition, the paper or magnetic tape output of the computer containing the "text" to be printed, as well as pre-programmed instructions concerning page make-up, character width, typefaces, justification, etc., is used to activate either a hot-metal typesetting device or a photo-composer.

The most frequently cited disadvantages of computer printouts as a basis for photo-offset reproduction are poor legibility and higher production costs resulting from the lower density of text storage on the page. In contrast, computer composition combined with photo-offset makes possible the use of a great variety of typefaces and type sizes. It produces better typographic quality and allows for greater flexibility in page makeup.

A number of general-purpose and special-purpose computers can be used for composition. Special-purpose computers can perform line justification as well as automatic or semi-automatic hyphenation control. Hyphenation may be based on a combination of logic and dictionary look-up, on logic only, or on guessing when logic fails. The simplest model stops whenever it reaches a point at which a word must be hyphenated, to allow a human to decide where the hyphen should go.

In the case of the general-purpose computers, software must include such composition functions as format and typography control, justification, hyphenation and page makeup. Specifications concerning line widths, indentation, type fonts, italicizing, bold-facing, subscripts, spacing between lines, etc. must be included in the computer programs.

For horizontal and vertical justification, the program must specify the spacing between lines, the width of lines, the width of each character in each of the type fonts used, and the range of word spacing that will be permitted. On the basis of this information, when, for example, the computer comes to a word or part of a word that will not fit into the specified line width, it will carry the word to the next line and will increase the spaces between the words to fill the preceding line. A whole paragraph may be rearranged in this manner when the objective is to avoid hyphenation.

The majority of computer-controlled typesetting operations use a combination of logic and dictionary look-up for hyphenation. When the computer reaches a word that must be hyphenated it first checks a stored dictionary of words with hyphens in all possible positions. If the word is there, the computer chooses the hyphenating position that places the line within the specified justification limits. If the word is not found in the dictionary then the computer applies the rules of logic stored in its memory. If it does not have rules of logic the computer may arbitrarily place the hyphen after an odd numbered letter, based on statistics that in the English language most hyphens fall after the third, fifth, seventh, etc. letter in a word. The need for hyphenation can be reduced or eliminated through appropriate instructions for line justification, specifically by allowing a greater range of word and character spacing within the line.

The proofreading operation, which is to detect errors other than those which occurred during human keyboarding, can be somewhat of a problem when computer typesetting is combined with photocomposition. To produce the equivalent of conventional galley proofs for this operation the expensive process of making a copy from the film output of the photocomposer must be used.[7]

The production of <u>Index Medicus</u> is an example of the application of computer composition combined with phototypesetting.

Microfilm Output

A computer output microfilm (COM) is a third generation output device that accepts digital output from the computer, converts it to analog signals and prints in on microfilm at rates from 25,000 to 100,000 characters per second. Depending on the model a COM unit may print alphanumerics, graphics, or both, can vary character size and style and can act as a high-speed non-impact printer.

Several COM units operate both on-line and off-line, but most frequently microfilm is produced off-line from the magnetic tape output of the computer. As the tape is read the logic section of the COM device translates the incoming signals as data handling commands and directs the data display unit to present the data in the programmed format to the microfilm, where it is recorded. There are two methods to present data for photographing into microfilm. In most units data are displayed one character at a time on the face of a cathode ray tube and photographed onto microfilm by a microfilm camera. In the other method the microfilm frame is located in a near vacuum in front of an electron beam gun, and character-generating circuits are activated to generate analog signals that deflect an electron beam in the recorder to form images, directly, one at a time on the microfilm. [8]

Computer output microfilming in an off-line situation is similar to computer composition in the sense that in the former the digital output of the computer is used to create microfilm and in the latter it is used to produce photographic film for offset reproduction.

Voice Output

Voice output systems may be based on analog recording of voice or on digitally controlled synthesis of speech.

In the simplest voice response systems a limited number of words or phrases are pre-recorded. These may be analog recordings or the words and phrases may be stored as a set of numbers representing analog signals that are converted back into sound for output.

Two major types of computer controlled voice synthesizer have been developed experimentally. One consists of an electronic analog of the human speech organ or vocal tract, the other simulates the sounds of human speech but not the vocal tract that produces them. [5]

Because of their limited vocabulary, voice output units are suitable for applications in which immediate replies to telephone inquiries are needed to answer very specific questions from a highly formatted file. Examples of this type of data are stock market quotations, answers to queries in a bank concerning loans, mortgages, status of accounts, etc., and inventory information in a manufacturing facility.

Storage

The function of the storage unit of the computer is to store the data, the program, the intermediate and final results before output, and any other information related to the problem being processed.

Information in the computer is represented as finite sequences of digits which are stored in physical devices called registers. The sequence of digits stored in a register is called a word. A number of different physical devices may be used as registers. A register may be composed of an array of magnetic cores, of a group of magnetic spots on the layers of a thin magnetic film unit, or of magnetized spots on a magnetic drum, among other devices.

The number of digits that are stored in a register defines both the length of the register and the length of the word stored in it. Depending upon its design, the computer may operate entirely upon words of fixed length, entirely on words of variable length, or on a combination of both.

Fixed and variable word lengths describe the smallest unit of information that can be addressed and processed by a computer. In a variable word length operation the smallest unit of information is a character. In a fixed word length operation information is addressed and handled in words containing a predetermined number of characters.

According to its function every register in a digital computer belongs to one or several of the following groups:

    Input/output registers;
    Storage registers;
    Control registers;
    Arithmetic registers.

Computer Hardware and Software 113

Every register has two basic properties: a read property and a write property.

The read property means that when information is taken from a register its contents remain unaltered. The write property means that when information is entered in a register it will replace the register's previous contents.

Every storage register has a third property: that it is uniquely identifiable by an individual location number which is called its address. This numerical address enables the programmer to specify to the computer exactly where to locate a given instruction or a given piece of information. Information stored in addressable locations is accessible, can be referred to, and can be replaced. All addressable registers have associated with them a sequence of digits representing their content and another set of digits representing their address. [9]

Storage Devices

Storage may be either main storage or auxiliary storage. Main storage accepts information from the input unit, exchanges information with the control and the logical/arithmetic unit, and can furnish information to the output unit.

When necessary, the capacity of main storage can be increased through the use of an auxiliary or secondary storage unit. Auxiliary storage is not directly accessible to the central processing unit or input and output devices; all information to and from auxiliary storage must go through main storage.

Document retrieval applications frequently require the use of high capacity auxiliary storage devices because of the large amounts of alphabetic information that may be involved. For this reason magnetic tape and disk storage are important in these applications.

Storage devices can be also differentiated in terms of the type of access they provide. Magnetic core will allow random access; disk, drum, and data cell storage will allow direct access to the location of the desired information. Magnetic tape provides serial access, which means that searching must start at the beginning of the tape and continue sequentially until the desired record is reached. Speed of access is another important characteristic of storage devices and has direct bearing on the efficiency and cost of computer systems. For example, core storage provides the shortest access time and, while it is the most expensive storage device in terms of cost per storage location, it may be, in some cases, the most economical in terms of cost per machine calculation.

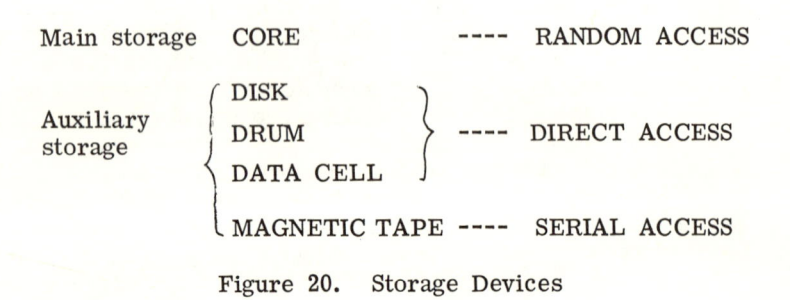

Main storage   CORE   ---- RANDOM ACCESS

Auxiliary storage { DISK, DRUM, DATA CELL } ---- DIRECT ACCESS

MAGNETIC TAPE ---- SERIAL ACCESS

Figure 20. Storage Devices

Core storage

    Magnetic cores used for main storage are made up of tiny ferromagnetic rings (cores) strung on screens of wires called planes. Cores can be magnetized by sending electrical current through the appropriate wires. The direction of the current will determine the polarity of the magnetic state of the core, with the two states used to represent 0 and 1. The storage device is so designed that any single core can be selected for writing or reading without affecting any other.

    Since the storage device is made up of an array of planes, the number of cores in each plane and the number of planes will determine storage capacity. For example, if each plane is 128 cores wide and 128 cores long, then the total number of cores per plane will be 128 x 128 = 16,384. If there are 70 planes, then the total storage capacity will be 70 x 128 x 128 = 1,146,880 bits. At seven bits per character the total character storage capacity of the unit is 1,146,880 /7 = 163,840 characters.

Computer Hardware and Software 115

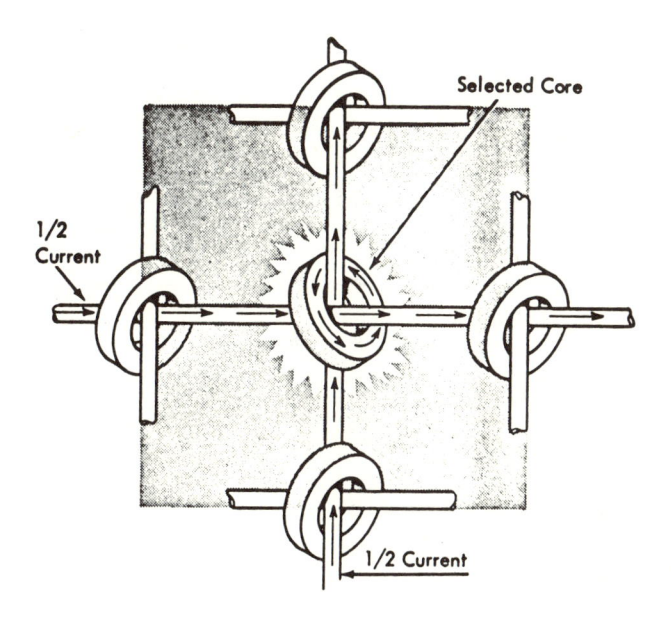

Figure 21. Selecting a Core

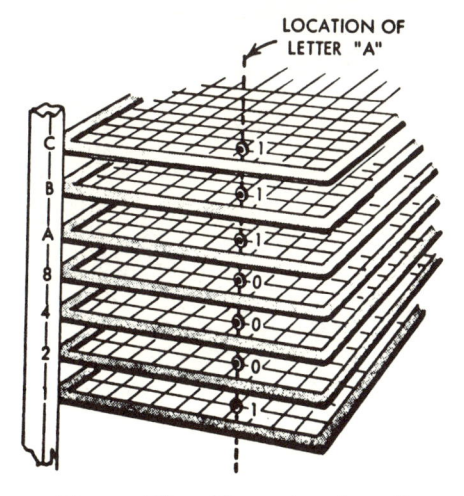

Figure 22. Character Location

Disk Storage

A magnetic disk is a thin disk coated on both sides with magnetic material. In a typical unit 25 disks are mounted on a vertical revolving shaft with enough room between them to provide space for the read/write heads. The read/write heads are mounted on arms that move horizontally between the disks. Each arm has two read/write heads, one for the bottom surface of the upper disk and one for the top surface of the lower disk.

Data are stored in the form of magnetized spots on concentric tracks on each surface of the disk. Each track contains a number of directly addressable locations. Information is accessible by specifying the disk surface, the track number, and the location on the track. Some computers use interchangeable disk packs which can be removed and stored in the same manner as reels of tape are stored. Disk storage units provide extremely high storage capacity, ranging up to millions of characters.

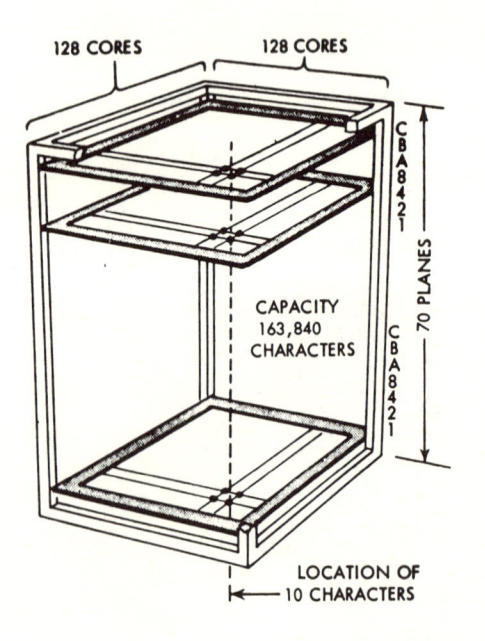

Figure 23. Schematic, 163,840 Position Storage

Computer Hardware and Software 117

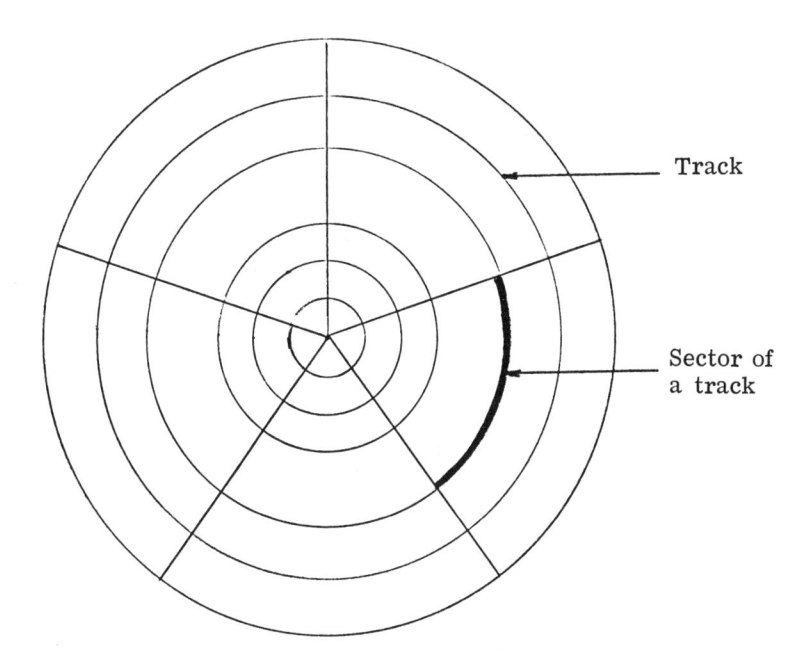

Figure 24. Information Arrangement on Disk

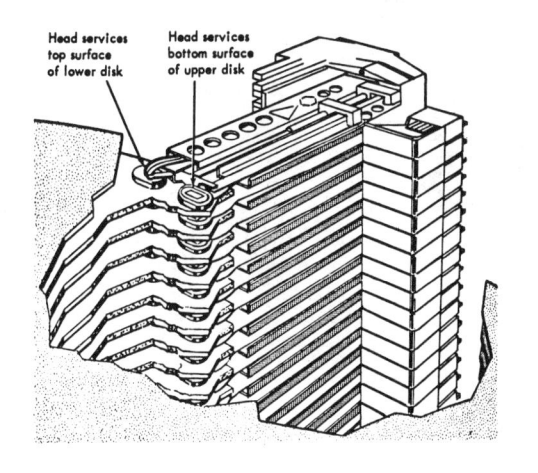

Figure 25. Head Arrangement, Disk Storage

Magnetic Drum Storage

The magnetic drum is a constant speed rotating cylinder whose outer surface is coated with magnetic material. Information is recorded on the drum surface in the form of magnetic spots by read/write heads that are suspended a very slight distance from the surface of the drum. Each drum has a specific number of addressable storage locations. The capacity of each storage location varies with the design of the drum and the data representation code used. Because reading occurs when a specific location is passing under the heads, access time may vary depending upon the distance to be traveled by the addressed location to the read/write head.[2]

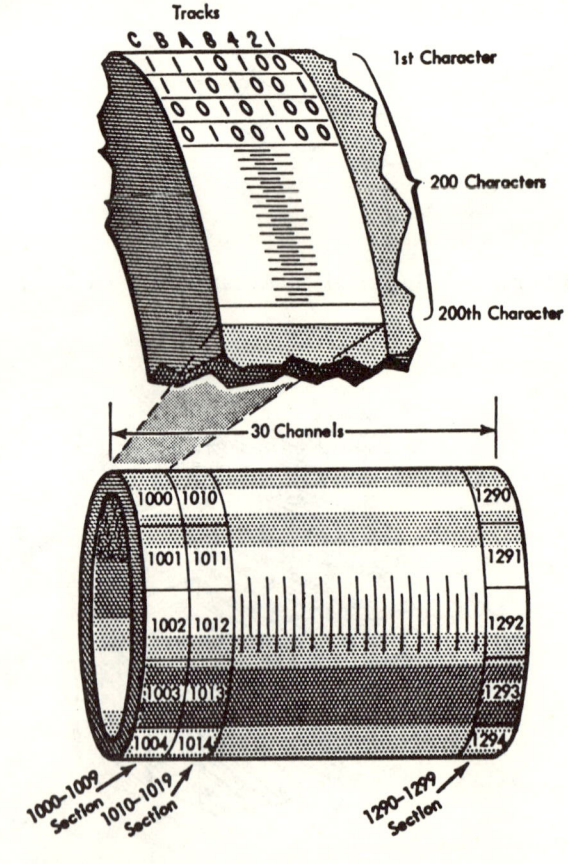

Figure 26. Schematic of Drum Storage

Data Cells

Data cells are made up of thin strips of magnetic film, several of which are grouped together to constitute a sub-cell. Several cells in turn make up a data cell drive. The IBM 2321 Data Cell Drive, for example, has 10 cells per drive and 20 sub-cells per cell. The sub-cells contain 2 x 12 inch strips and information is stored on the 200 tracks available on each 2 x 12 inch strip. Each strip can be accessed directly and a cell may be removed and replaced by others. Each data cell drive has the capacity of storing 40 million characters.[2]

Programming Languages

The sequence of steps to be performed by the computer to accomplish a given job must be translated into explicit and detailed instructions that the computer can follow. This series of instructions is called a program and the notation in which it is written is called a programming language.

The program must define in complete detail what the computer is to do with the data that are fed into it, under every conceivable combination of circumstances. One instruction may tell what operation to perform and where to locate the data on which to perform it; another will tell what to do with the results. The computer refers to the instructions sequentially and it can be instructed to repeat, modify or skip certain instruction, depending on intermediate results.

The steps required before the actual preparation of the program can begin are: definition of the problem, analysis of the operation, and flow charting. These steps are usually carried out without reference to any particular computer or to any programming language.

Programming languages can be classified as belonging to one of the following categories:

Machine languages;
Symbolic or assembly languages;
Problem-oriented or high-level languages.

Machine and symbolic or assembly languages are machine-dependent because they are designed for a specific computer. Problem-oriented languages are largely independent of the machine; it is advantageous, however, for the programmer to have some familiarity with the computer for which he is writing the program.

Writing a program in machine language is a difficult and tedious process because the program must be written in machine coding for a particular machine and because the full burden of organization of the program and of the logic to be used is placed directly on the programmer. To overcome the problems inherent in machine language programming, symbolic or assembly languages were introduced. The primary advantages of symbolic programming over machine language programming are the use of symbolic notation, the automatic assignment of addresses for both instructions and data, and the use of macro-instructions. While one symbolic instruction usually corresponds to one machine language instruction, macro-instructions generate a sequence of machine language instructions. Thus, in symbolic programming the clerical task of programming is significantly reduced. The programmer, however, still must consider the particular computer to be programmed, that is, his program is machine-dependent.

Perhaps the most widely used programming languages in current use are problem-oriented languages. Programming in a high level problem-oriented language makes the programmer to a very large extent independent of the machine. In contrast with machine languages or assembly languages that need to take into consideration the structure and organization of particular computers, high-level problem-oriented languages reflect the structure and organization of the problem area. One instruction in a program written in a problem-oriented language usually corresponds to several instructions in the corresponding machine language program. This greatly reduces the number of instructions to be written by the programmer. This fact, together with the simplicity of problem-oriented languages, and the fact that the programmer needs to know relatively little about the structure and organization of the computer, is an important advantage of problem-oriented languages. [9]

Before it can be used for actual processing a program written in a symbolic or a problem-oriented language must be translated into the machine language of the particu-

Computer Hardware and Software 121

lar computer being used. This is accomplished by loading the translator program or processor into core memory, along with the program as written by the programmer. The computer then automatically translates the programmer's instructions into instructions in machine language. Programs written in a language other than a machine language are called source programs, and the result of the translation is a machine language program called the object program.

The processor that will translate symbolic instructions into machine language is called an assembler or assembly program. The processor program which is used in the translation of a program written in a problem-oriented language is called a compiler.

It should be noted that the processor is a machine language program that is tied to a particular computer and that it translates a source program into an object program for that same computer.

Examples of problem-oriented languages are FORTRAN, ALGOL, COBOL, and PL/1. FORTRAN (FORmula TRANslation) and ALGOL (ALGOrithmic Language) are designed primarily for the solution of mathematical, scientific, and engineering problems. COBOL (COmmon Business Oriented Language) is designed for business oriented applications. FORTRAN and COBOL are very similar in their basic concepts. One of the main differences between them is in the language that the programmer uses. Where business English is used by COBOL, mathematical language is used in FORTRAN.

A relatively recently developed language is PL/1 (Programming Language, version 1). It combines some of the features of ALGOL, FORTRAN, and COBOL and has other features that are alien to all three. It was developed to meet the need for a broad-base language that may be used for a variety of problems. PL/1 has the ability to handle problems that require the processing of data represented by characters, words, or symbols. Its capability to handle characters as individual symbols or as strings makes the language extremely useful for the processing of the type of non-numerical information that is frequently involved in information science problems. [10]

SNOBOL and COMIT are examples of programming languages that have been developed primarily for the proc-

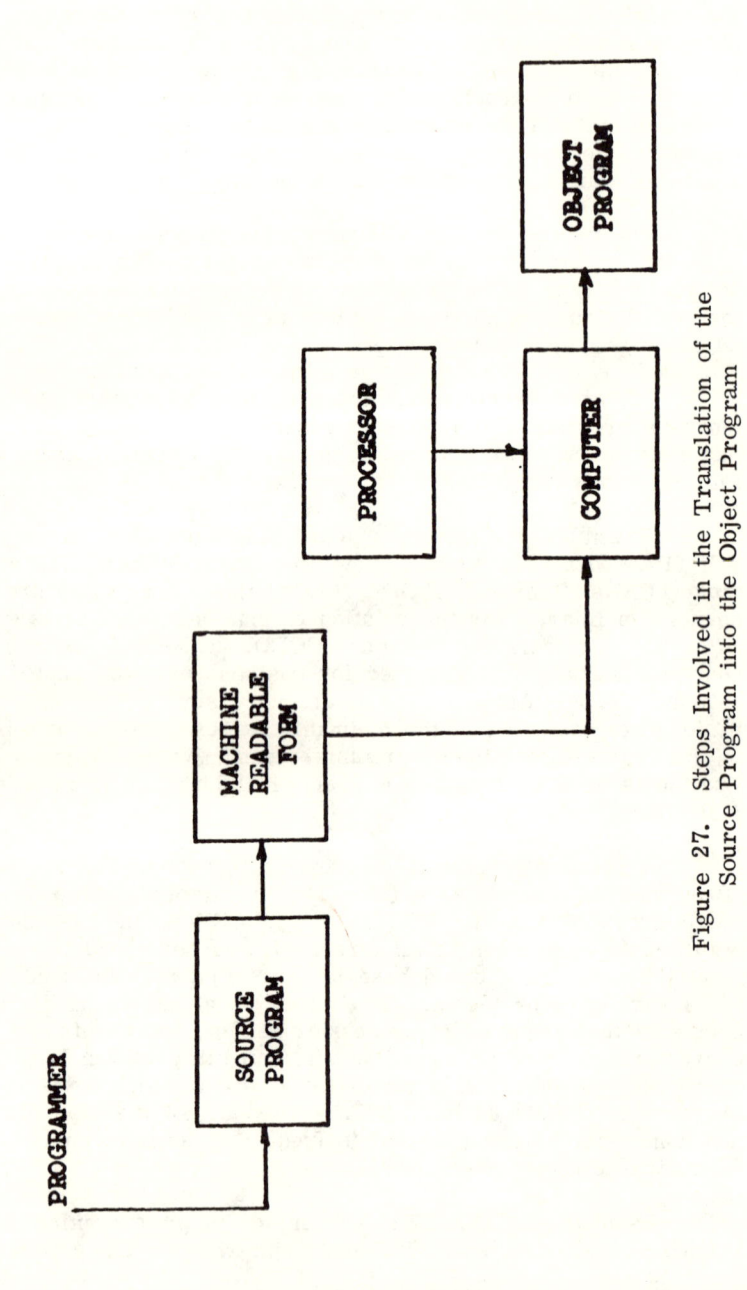

Figure 27. Steps Involved in the Translation of the Source Program into the Object Program

essing of non-numerical information. Both are user-oriented symbol manipulation languages. SNOBOL, developed at Bell Telephone Laboratories, is designed for the manipulation of strings of characters. COMIT was developed at the Massachusetts Institute of Technology, primarily for programming mechanical translation problems.

Computer Time-Sharing

The technique called time-sharing is a significant development in computer technology, with potential for information retrieval applications. Time-sharing provides a number of users with direct access to a single computer from remote terminals. In contrast to the normal batch-processing approach, it permits each user to interact with the computer on a real time basis.

In conventional batch-processing, computing jobs are submitted to an operator to be processed sequentially and when each job is completed the results are returned to the user. This mode of operation has two major drawbacks from the user's point of view:

1) It denies direct access to the computer and does not allow the user to interact with the computer, and

2) It denies immediate access to the computer because the time required for the user's program to be processed and the results returned to him may involve hours or even days.

Allowing each user to be on-line so as to get immediate response from the computer enables him to modify his program during its execution. By guaranteeing each user direct access to the computer, with delays so small that he does not notice them, time-sharing gives him the small units of computer time that he actually uses immediately and in such a manner that he can interact with the computer.

In batch-processing the computer is used to execute algorithms, explicit procedures, very rapidly and accurately. The heuristic contributions are made by human problem solvers before their programs get into the machine. In contrast with this type of use, on-line time-sharing permits interaction with the computer and thus allows a combination of the algorithmic and heuristic approaches to problem solving.

It provides feedback during the process of formulation of the problem while the computer is working on it, and it permits continuous redesign of the procedures. "To solve a problem effectively one must be able to move quickly forward from a hunch or hypothesis through definition of procedure to test, then back again either to revise the basic notion or to incorporate it into a larger structure of thought. Problem solving is a succession of such forward and backward excursions. The net movement must be forward, but the retreats are no less important than the advances."[11]

Because of these advantages the range of applications of man-computer interactive systems has been expanding rapidly. It goes beyond the scientific and engineering fields to include experimental applications in teaching and learning, in medicine, and in document retrieval. Project Intrex, the MAC Technical Information Project, SPIRES at Stanford University, and the State University of New York Biomedical Communications Network at the Upstate Medical Center, Syracuse, are examples of on-line, real time, user-oriented document retrieval systems. Two of these, Project Intrex and the MAC Technical Information Project, are described in detail in the section on representative machine applications.

Definition of Time-Sharing

In a time-sharing system many users share the time of the computer and have direct and concurrent access to it on what appears to be an exclusive and immediate basis. While access to the computer appears to be simultaneous, in reality the computer switches from one user to another. No noticeable delay is normally experienced by the user, however, because of the high speed of the computer and the relative slowness of humans and of input/output terminals.

Processing in a time-shared system is under the supervision of the executive or supervisory program which is permanently stored in computer memory. When it is a given user's turn to use processing time the executive program brings the appropriate material into core storage and works on it during the time allocated for that particular user. If the job is not completed during the allocated time the problem is put back into storage while the executive program attends to other users' problems. When it is the first user's turn again, his problem is brought back to be worked on further. The process is repeated until the problem is completed.

This type of processing involves <u>multiprogramming</u>, which means that several programs are maintained in an active state. The executive program handles addressing problems relating to the allocation of small fractions of main memory to any one program, shuffling data and programs in main memory and between main and auxiliary memory.

Each user program is assured of its chance to operate at least once in every nt seconds, where t is the maximum time interval for a program and n is the number of user programs in the system at any given time. It is also possible to introduce priorities into the system that will designate one program as more important than some others on the basis of such criteria as the relative importance of the job or the length of time it requires.

The increasing realization that frequently the limiting factor in on-line time-sharing is the sharing of the processor, rather than sharing of the memory, resulted in <u>multiprocessing</u>. Multiprocessing is achieved by using two or more processors in association with one or more common memory units and peripheral devices. This technique is especially useful in applications that require high reliability. If one processor malfunctions, its workload can be shifted to the others.

Because several users share the computer's memory it is important to provide a mechanism for the detection of materials stored in the memory which belong to a specific user and are out of bounds for other users who may request them. It is also necessary to notify the user at the console that he has requested stored material that is not available to him, so that he may make the required changes in his program. Access to materials outside a given user's bounds may violate privacy and might destroy another user's data.

Kinds of Time-Sharing

It is possible to distinguish among several kinds of time-sharing systems by whether they provide full language capabilities, restricted language capabilities, or whether they are dedicated (common data base) systems.

The general purpose time-sharing system attempts to provide the user with the full range of language capabilities and processing services which he would have if he were

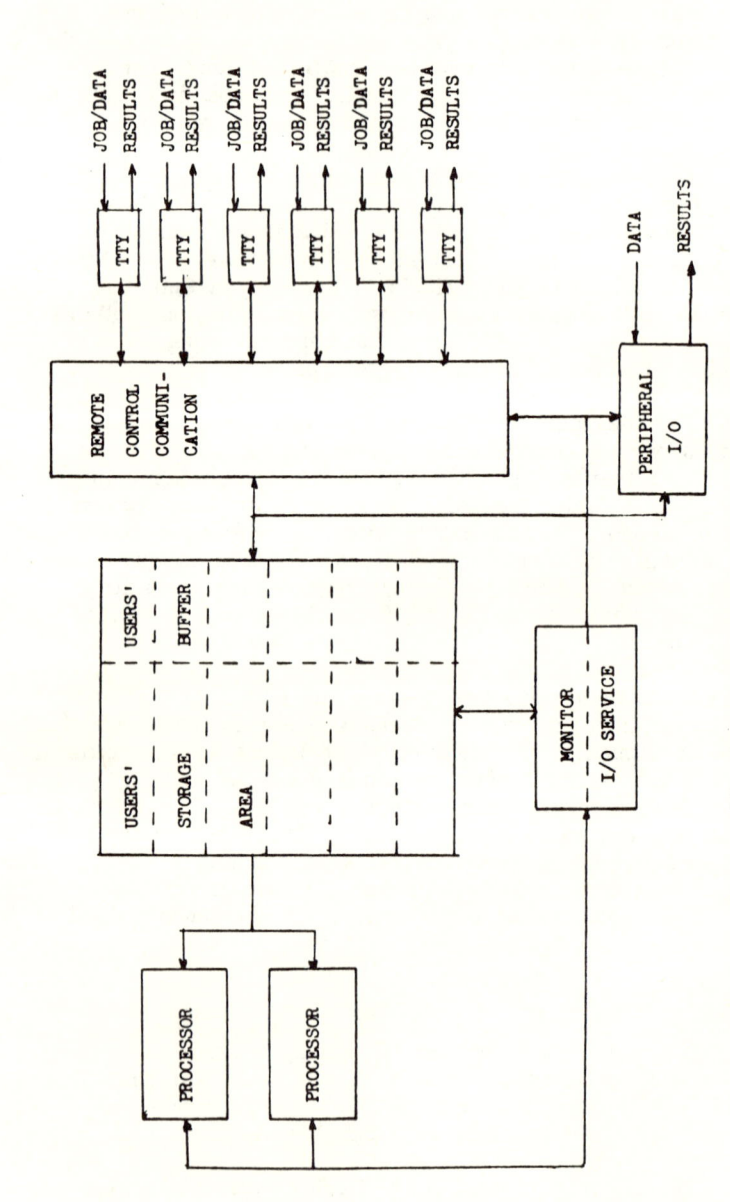

Figure 28. Block Diagram of the Computer as a Multiprogrammed Multiprocessing Time-Shared System

Computer Hardware and Software

the sole user of a general purpose computer. Perhaps the best known example of this kind of time-sharing system is the compatible time-sharing system at the Massachusetts Institute of Technology.

A second type of time-sharing system restricts the language capabilities of the user, permitting him to work in only one specific problem area using one particular language. Examples of such special purpose time-sharing systems are IBM's QUIKTRAN system, which uses a simplified FORTRAN language, and the Rand Corporation's JOSS system.

The third type of time-sharing system is the dedicated or common data base system in which the user can pose only a restricted class of acceptable questions about the data base and can solve only certain recurrent problems for which solution methods have already been provided by the system. A well known example of this approach is American Airlines' SABRE reservation system which allows ticket agents at more than 1,000 different consoles to interact with the same central data file simultaneously.

Terminals

In a time-sharing system, terminals provide the means of communication between the remote user and the computer, for both input and output.

The simplest and most commonly used terminals are teletype terminals on which the user types in his program and/or data and receives his reply from the computer in hard copy form typed out by the teletype machine. More sophisticated terminals provide a visual display of both input and output information on a cathode ray tube (CRT) screen. On this type of video terminal, information for input is typed on a keyboard and displayed on the cathode ray tube screen for visual accuracy check. Before the data are released to the computer, the operator can backspace and correct or erase the information. Information received from the computer is also displayed on the screen. The IBM 2772 Data Communication System, for example, employs a 14-inch square cathode ray tube screen for its display unit, on which up to 960 characters can be displayed. Character format can consist of 12 lines of 80 characters each, or 15 lines of 64 characters each. Character size depends on the format chosen. In addition to displaying alpha-numeric information, some display units can present tables, graphs, and charts on the cathode ray tube screen.

Since it is frequently desirable to obtain hard copy of the output message, video terminals can be equipped with printers. The IBM 2772 Data Communication System, for example, can be equipped with a printer that prints up to 66 characters per second and up to 132 characters per line. Devices that are capable of producing hard copy directly from the cathode ray tube display at a relatively low cost are still largely in the developmental stage.

To provide for further flexibility, data communication systems may have additional optional components that will allow them to accept for input and to produce for output cards, paper tape, or magnetic tape, or to operate in a remote batch mode. In the last case, data for batch processing are transmitted to the computer via a terminal, not for immediate processing but to be entered in the queue of jobs that are waiting to be batch processed.

Figure 29. Video Terminal

Human Factors in Time-Sharing

The emergence of computer time-sharing systems and the resulting developments raise some interesting questions relating to the human engineering problems involved in the use of this type of system. Implicit in time-sharing is the opportunity and need for extensive interaction between computers and persons of various disciplines and backgrounds. The degree to which human factors are considered in the design of time-sharing systems will determine how symbiotic or synergetic man-computer interaction will be.

Examples of human engineering problems are the design of command languages, system response time, ease of use, conflicting needs of novices and experienced users, and operational trade-offs. Relatively little research has been done relating to the nature of man-computer interaction in a time-sharing environment and the factors that affect the quality or productivity of those interactions.

Time-sharing implies a dialogue between the user and the computer. Man communicates data and instructions and the computer communicates results. Involved in the man-computer dialogue are user-oriented conversational languages and we need to know more about the psychological principles that should guide their design.

The effect of response time on the user is another interesting problem. Response time is the time required to complete a command and to output the results. Generally the objective in systems design has been to minimize response time, assuming that the user will benefit from this. However, in a minimum response time system, response time will be of variable length, and the effect of variable response time on the user is being studied by some researchers.

Ease of use, an important objective for any time-sharing system, raises the problem of designing a system that the beginner can learn to use easily on the basis of the system's built-in teaching capability, and that will, at the same time, make it possible for the experienced user, for whom some of the feedback represents unnecessary delays, to by-pass some of the teaching steps.

Operational trade-offs relating to time-sharing systems concern two conflicting objectives--to provide for maximum accessibility to the system for the user and at the same time minimize the time that the system is idle. The two objectives conflict because maximum access implies limiting the number of users, which in turn may mean idle time except when all users are on-line at once. Optimization in this case is partly an economic problem and partly a psychological one--there is a limit to the cost of idle time that the system can tolerate and there is also a limit to the number of times that the user will tolerate being refused immediate access to the system.[12]

References

1. Shannon, Claude. "A Symbolic Analysis of Relay and Switching Circuits," Transactions of the American Institute of Electrical Engineers, 57:713-723, 1938.

2. Introduction to IBM Data Processing Systems Student Text. 2nd ed., International Business Machines Corporation, 1968.

3. Stender, Robert C. "The Future Role of Keyboards in Data Entry," Datamation, 16:60-72, June 1970.

4. Rabinow, Jacob C. "Whither OCR?" Datamation, 15:38-42, July 1969.

5. Weitzman, Coy. "Voice Recognition and Response Systems," Datamation, 15:165-170, December 1969.

6. Meadow, Charles T. Man-Machine Communication. New York, Wiley, 1970.

7. Walter, Gerard O. "Typesetting," Scientific American, 220:61-69, May 1969.

8. Yerkes, Charles P. "Microfilm--A New Dimension for Computers," Datamation, 16:94-97, December 1969.

9. Dimitry, Donald L. and Thomas H. Mott, Jr. Introduction to FORTRAN IV Programming. New York, Holt, Rinehart and Winston, 1966.

10. Mott, Thomas H., Susan Artandi, and Leny Struminger. Introduction to PL/1 Programming for Library and

Information Science. New York, Academic Press. (In press)

11. Licklider, J. C. R. "Man-Computer Partnership," International Science and Technology, May 1965, pp. 18-26.

12. Nickerson, Raymond S., Jerome L. Elkinol and Jaine R. Carbonell. "Human Factors in the Design of Time Sharing Computer Systems," Human Factors, 10:127-134, April 1968.

CHAPTER 6

REPRESENTATIVE MACHINE APPLICATIONS

Introduction

Mechanical Retrieval of Manually Organized Information Combined with the Production of a File for Manual Searching
- EXAMPLES:
  - MEDLARS System
  - MARC System

Production of a File for Manual Searching from Mechanically Organized Information
- EXAMPLE: KWIC Index

Mechanical Matching of Manually Created Interest Profiles with Manually Created Document Surrogates
- EXAMPLE: Selective Dissemination of Information (SDI)

On-Line Retrieval of Manually Organized Information
- EXAMPLES:
  - Project Intrex
  - MAC Technical Information Project

Production of Printed Indexes

Automatic Indexing

Machine Translation

INTRODUCTION

Most computer-based document retrieval systems currently in operation provide for the mechanical searching of manually organized information. The document representations created through human intellectual effort are stored in some kind of a file that can be searched mechanically.

These single purpose systems, which were designed exclusively around this kind of machine search capability and were operated on a batch-processing basis, evolved into systems that combine the capacity for mechanical searching with the capability of producing--from the same file--a tool for manual searching, such as a printed index or printed cards. MEDLARS, at the National Library of Medicine, which produces Index Medicus for manual searching, is an example of a computer system that serves this dual purpose. Many of the systems of this type use direct files, on magnetic tape, which are searched sequentially. As files increase in size, however, sequential access becomes less practical and new approaches are being sought.

Another variation of the manually organized, machine searchable system operates on real-time and is used on-line by the user through a remote terminal. Machine searching combined with access through terminals and based on time-sharing is a relatively new development which is in the center of current interest. It is regarded by some as the answer for the future. At the present time the successful implementation of this type of system hinges on such factors as hardware development (primarily the development of terminals), on reduction in cost, and on the clarification of human engineering and management problems related to the use of terminals. The MAC Project at M.I.T. is an early example of access through terminals to a time-shared computer. Project Intrex, also at M.I.T., is currently experimenting with a machine searchable library catalog which is queried and produces output through cathode ray tube terminals.

In some applications the computer is used solely for the preparation of tools for manual searching, with no system requirement for mechanical search capability. These systems are usually intended to produce such things as book catalogs, printed indexes or printed catalog or index cards. In systems in which these printed tools are based on manual indexing the capabilities of the computer are utilized to a limited extent only--primarily for the ordering and arranging of entries or to activate a typesetting device. In other systems the computer is used in a more sophisticated way. In a KWIC index, for example, the computer generates index entries automatically from the titles of documents and then arranges them in the order desired for manual searching.

Other information-oriented computer applications include selective dissemination of information (SDI), automatic indexing and abstracting and automatic translation. Library management-oriented applications such as the computerization of circulation routines, ordering of publications, etc., are interesting, but they will not be discussed here.

A number of representative computer applications will be described in detail in the section that follows. The systems that are described were selected as illustrations of particular types of computer applications, and no attempt is made to be all inclusive or to give a comprehensive critical evaluation.

MECHANICAL RETRIEVAL OF MANUALLY ORGANIZED INFORMATION COMBINED WITH THE PRODUCTIONS OF A FILE FOR MANUAL SEARCH

General Diagram

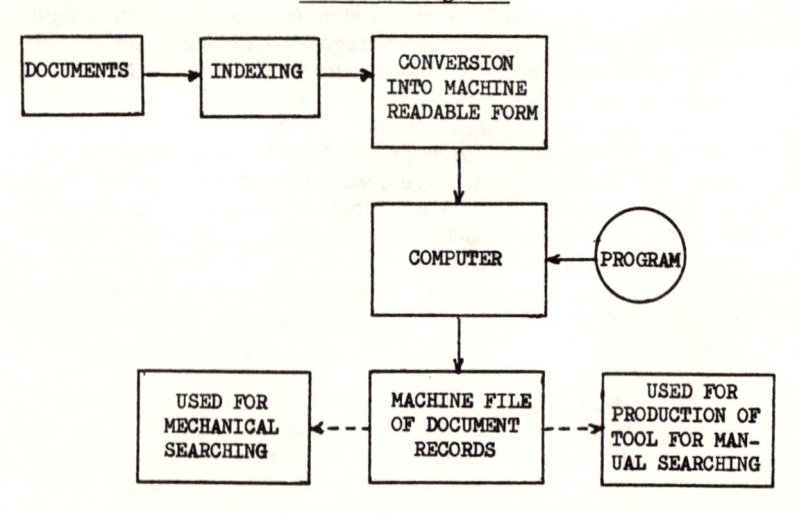

Figure 30.

Examples: MEDLARS System
             MARC System

The MEDLARS System

In the MEDLARS System (Medical Literature Analysis and Retrieval System) at the National Library of Medicine, documents are indexed by people. The resulting document descriptions, with their associated document references, are organized in a machine searchable file serving several purposes. The file can be searched mechanically in response to specific information queries, and printed indexes (Index Medicus, Bibliography of Medical Reviews, etc.) are produced from it for manual searching. In addition to these two applications, portions of the MEDLARS file are currently used in experimentation with an on-line remote access retrieval system.

While the MEDLARS System in its present form is relatively new--it became operational in January 1964--it represents the continuation of bibliographic activities in the field of medicine which date back to 1879 when the original Index Medicus was started. The MEDLARS files contain citations to articles in about 2,300 of the more important biomedical journals of the world published since January 1964. Most journals are indexed cover-to-cover, with the exception of those that are not exclusively medical; these journals are indexed selectively for their biomedical coverage only. Of the 2,300 journals indexed, one third is indexed exhaustively at an average of ten terms per article, and the rest less exhaustively at an average of four terms per article. The overall average depth of indexing is 6.7 terms per article.

In 1970 the MEDLARS data base included about one million citations, and about 200,000 citations are added annually. Most of the citations are to journal articles but some refer to technical reports. Approximately 50% of the articles are in languages other than English. Duplicate MEDLARS files on magnetic tape have been made available to a number of major medical libraries, such as the Universities of California (Los Angeles), Colorado, Alabama, Michigan and Harvard University.

Indexing

In the MEDLARS system indexing is based on a controlled vocabulary of Medical Subject Headings (MeSH) that was developed through the joint effort of professionals experienced in the indexing of biomedical literature, of the users of Index Medicus and MEDLARS, and of advisory panels composed of physicians and biomedical scientists. Medical Subject Headings contains about 8000 index terms. The indexing vocabulary also includes about 60 subheadings, terms that are used only in combination with other terms. Examples of subheadings are Anatomy, Histology, and Diagnosis.

In actual indexing MEDLARS indexers have access to a more extensive in-house vocabulary than the published version of MeSH. The in-house vocabulary is revised quarterly and includes geographical and provisional headings.

Not every index term included in the machine record appears in the printed Index Medicus because the machine record is intended to provide for more exhaustive indexing than the printed index used for manual searching. The subject headings that appear in Index Medicus, referred to as "print" terms or "Index Medicus" terms, are those which, in the indexer's judgment, cover the principal points of the article. The "non print" or "non Index Medicus" terms assigned to the document can be utilized only in the machine searches. This feature and the capability for Boolean and generic searching provide for greater flexibility of searching in the machine file than is possible in the printed Index Medicus.

The vocabulary of the system has been criticized as being unsatisfactory from the point of view of completeness, i.e. deficiency of terms in certain areas. The two major types of index-language problems identified by the recent MEDLARS evaluation study[1] are (1) lack of specificity of terms, and (2) ambiguous or spurious relationship between

JTA:			ARTICLES	INDEXER	REVISER
A - anonymous	PAGINATION				OPT. PAGINATION
D - non-std. date		318-24			
P - non-std. pagination					
AUTHOR DATA (print)					
AUTHOR DATA (sort)					
TITLE (English or English Translation)					
TITLE (Vernacular or Transliterated Vernacular)					

IM	NIM	MAIN HEADING *subheading	NO.	ENTRY VOCABULARY
		REVIEW (References)	1	
		ENGLISH ABSTRACT	2	
			3	
X		SPUTUM *cytology	4	
X		CARCINOMA, BRONCHOGENIC *diagnosis	5	
		BRONCHIAL NEOPLASMS *radiography	6	
X		BRONCHIAL NEOPLASMS *diagnosis	7	
		CARCINOMA, BRONCHOGENIC *radiography	8	
		CYTODIAGNOSIS	9	
		BRONCHIAL NEOPLASMS *pathology	10	
		BRONCHOSCOPY	11	
		CARCINOMA, EPIDERMOID *pathology	12	
X		LUNG NEOPLASMS *diagnosis	13	
		ADENOCARCINOMA *pathology	14	
		CARCINOMA, BRONCHOGENIC *pathology	15	
		BIOPSY	16	
			17	INPUT TYPIST: DISREGARD TERMS BELOW
		TIME FACTORS	18	
			19	
			20	
			21	
			22	
			23	
			24	
			25	

IM	NIM	CHECK TAGS	NIM	CHECK TAGS	NIM	CHECK TAGS	NIM	CHECK TAGS
		PREGNANCY		CATS		HISTORICAL BIOGRAPHY		CURRENT BIO-OBIT
		INFANT, NEWBORN (to 1 month)		CATTLE		HISTORICAL ARTICLE		ANIMAL EXPERIMENTS
		INFANT (1-23 months)		CHICK EMBRYO		ANCIENT	X	HUMAN
		CHILD, PRESCHOOL (2-5 years)		DOGS		MEDIEVAL	X	MALE
		CHILD (6-12 years)		FROGS		MODERN		FEMALE
		ADOLESCENCE (13-18 years)		GUINEA PIGS		15th CENT.		IN VITRO
		ADULT (19-44 years)		HAMSTERS		16th CENT.		CASE REPORT
		MIDDLE AGE (45-64 years)		MICE		17th CENT.		CLINICAL RESEARCH
	X	AGED (65- years)		MONKEYS		18th CENT.		COMPARATIVE STUDY
				RABBITS		19th CENT.	CITATION NO.	
				RATS		20th CENT.		

Figure 31. MEDLARS - Indexing Worksheet

terms. Activities to alleviate these deficiencies are currently in progress.

When the system was first mechanized, subheadings were replaced by such standard terms as Infant, Child, Aged, Biographies, Toxicological Report, etc. It appears, however, that assignment of such terms in addition to regular subject tags can cause false coordinations. For example, assuming that a given document describes "the use of penicillin in the treatment of colds of children and the use of streptomycin in the treatment of colds of the aged"-- then the following index topics could be assigned to the article:

    Penicillin   Aged
    Streptomycin   Therapy
    Child

Since there are no links in the system, Penicillin and Child, and Streptomycin and Aged would not be tied together in the index record. Thus, the document would be retrieved in response to both the inquiry concerning "the use of streptomycin in the treatment of children," and the one concerning "the use of penicillin in the treatment of the aged," as a result of false coordinations.

While some "check tags" of this type still remain in the system, subheadings were re-introduced into the vocabulary in January 1966 to increase the specificity of the main terms.

The MEDLARS system may be described as the combination of three subsystems:

    1) Input Subsystem;
    2) Retrieval Subsystem;
    3) Publication Subsystem.

Input Subsystem

In this part of the system, documents are analyzed by trained indexers who assign subject headings to them from the system's controlled vocabulary. Indexing decisions are recorded on worksheets, and basic unit records--consisting of bibliographic entry and index tags--are converted to machine-readable form through the preparation of punched paper

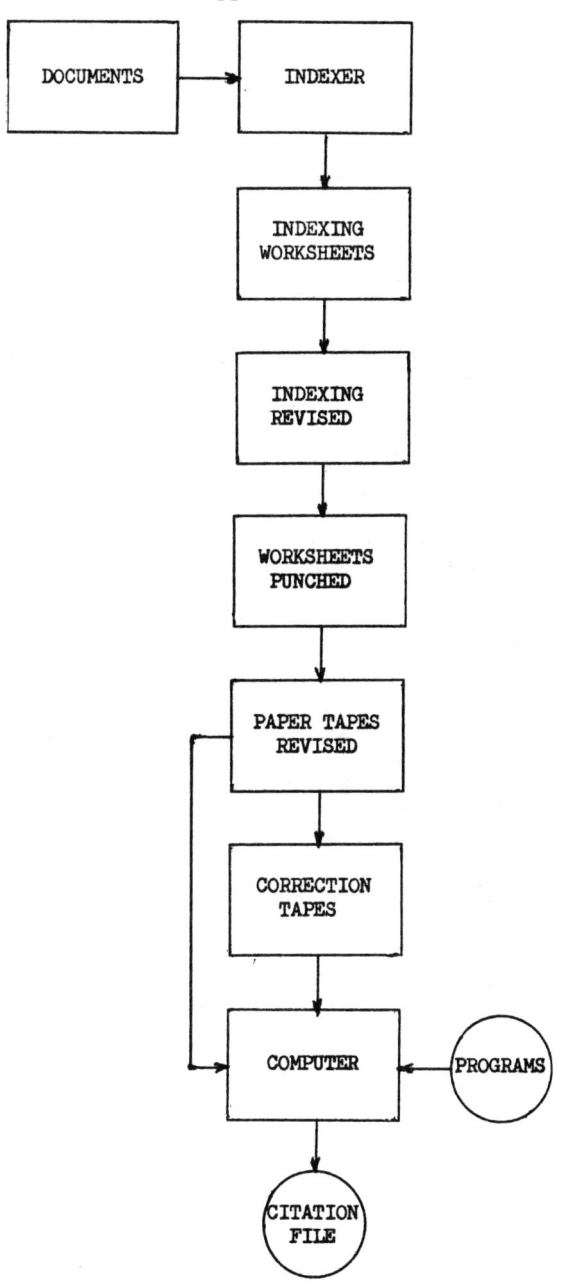

Figure 32. MEDLARS--Input Subsystem

tape. Hard copy produced simultaneously with the paper tape is proofread for accuracy and correction tapes are prepared when necessary. Input paper tapes and correction tapes go through a computer input procedure which transfers the input data for each document to magnetic tape.

The magnetic tape file produced by these input procedures contains unit records for each citation, arranged sequentially in accession number order. For each citation the following data are recorded: author, title (including English translation of foreign titles), journal reference, indication of language when other than English, and all index terms that were assigned to the document.

Retrieval Subsystem

The magnetic tape citation file is searched in response to specific information requests. Search requests are converted into search formulations, a description of the information requirement in the index language of the system. The retrieval file is a direct file and the citations, in input order, are searched sequentially on a coordinate basis. It is possible to ask for the presence or the absence of terms in many combinations in the description of a given document. After search formulations have been prepared they are converted into machine-readable form and are input to the computer. The citations that meet search requirements are recorded on magnetic tape, decoded into natural language, and printed on cards or paper by the computer. For greater efficiency in searching, queries are batched together and processed simultaneously.

It should be pointed out that in searching the computer does nothing more than match search formulations against indexed citations, or, putting it differently, it matches two lists, the longer list of citation records and the shorter list of query terms. Simultaneous processing of several queries means that a given record is matched against every query in the batch before the computer moves on to the next record (instead of checking each query separately against the entire file).

Publication Subsystem

In the publication subsystem printed indexes are gen-

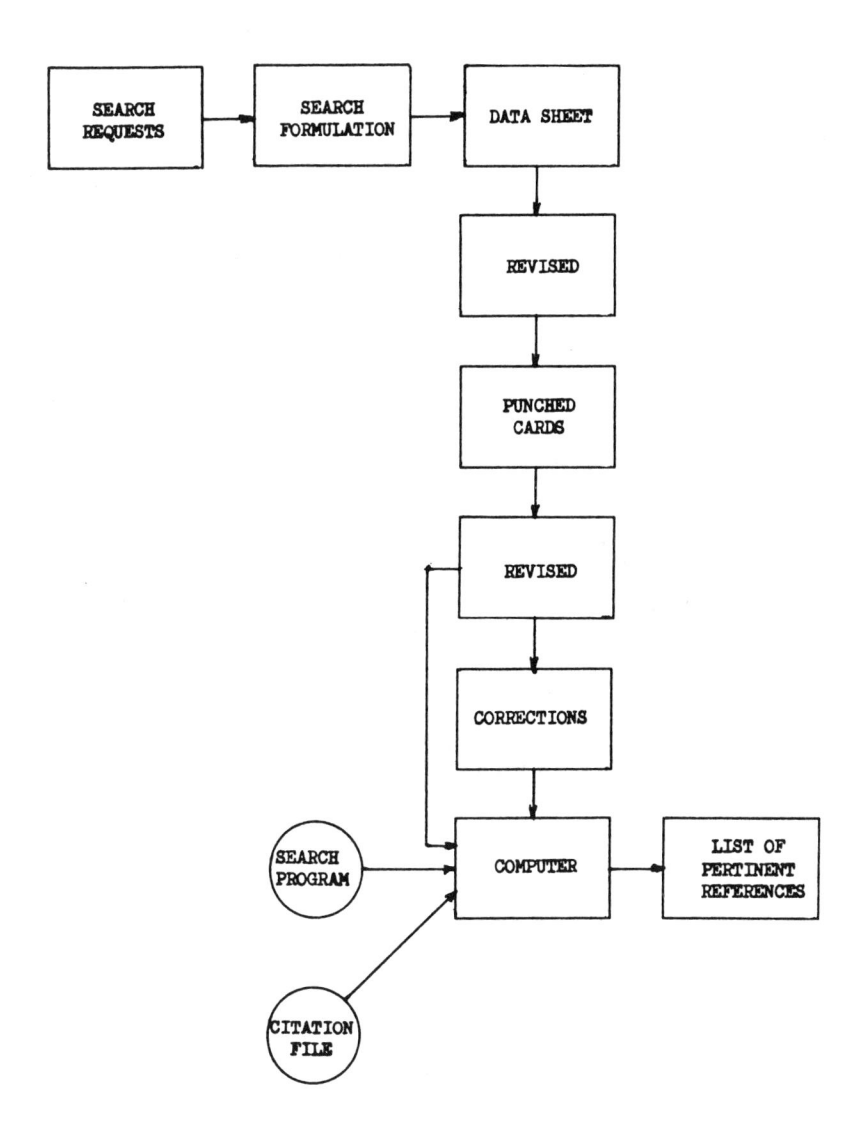

Figure 33. MEDLARS--Retrieval Subsystem

erated from the magnetic tape citation file. The computer program used in this process accomplish three major tasks:

1) Replication and sorting of citations under all the headings under which they are to be printed;

2) Formatting of each citation into standard print formats;

3) Photocomposition of the formatted tapes using a computer-driven photo-typesetter known as GRACE (Graphic Arts Composing Equipment).

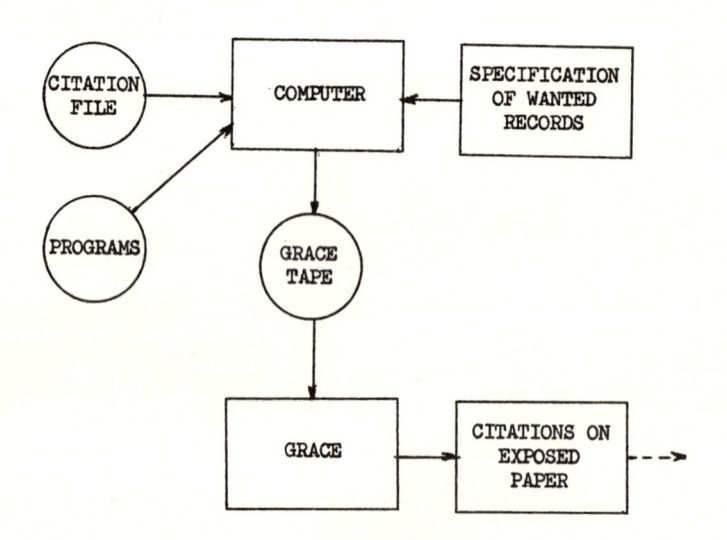

Figure 34. MEDLARS--Publication Subsystem

GRACE can use 226 different characters and prepares 23-centimeter-wide positive photographic film or paper. Character sets include a 6-point font of regular and boldfaced upper- and lower-case characters, a 10-point font of upper-case characters only, and a 14-point font of upper-case characters only. The final product of GRACE is a roll of exposed paper which is developed by an automatic processor.

The developed paper is inspected, cut into page-size sheets and sent to the printer for offset reproduction.[2]

On-line Retrieval

The National Library of Medicine is currently experimenting with extending its computerized information services to include the capability of searching the MEDLARS files on an on-line basis.

Two remote access systems are involved in experimentation with the MEDLARS data base: the State University of New York (SUNY) system and the AIM-TWX system. The SUNY system contains MEDLARS citations beginning from January 1967. The AIM-TWX system, developed by the Systems Development Corporation for the Lister Hill Center for Biomedical Communication of the National Library of Medicine, contains citations from the Abridged Index Medicus.[3] Both systems intend to explore the feasibility, effectiveness, utilization, and acceptance of an on-line biomedical information system.

Performance of the System

The recently completed MEDLARS evaluation study is significant not only because of the specific information it generated about the performance of the MEDLARS system but also, very importantly, because it represents the first large-scale evaluation of a major on-going computerized document retrieval system.

The principal objectives of the evaluation program were to study the requirements of demand search users, to get an objective measure of system performance in relation to those requirements, to discover factors that affect performance adversely, and to determine ways of satisfying user needs more efficiently or more economically, or both.

The prime requirements of demand search users were presumed to relate to the following factors: <u>coverage</u> of the literature by the system, the ability of the system to retrieve relevant documents (<u>recall power</u>), the ability of the system to withhold non-relevant documents (<u>precision power</u>), the <u>response time</u> of the system, the <u>format</u> in which the search results are presented, and the amount of <u>effort</u> the user must expend to get a satisfactory response from the system.

Over a substantial representative sample of MEDLARS requests the system was found to be operating on an average of 57.7% recall and 50.4% precision level. Failures were analyzed and found to be due to the following major factors: index language, indexing subsystem, searching subsystem, and inadequate interaction between requester and system.

Index language failures were caused by lack of specificity of terms and by ambiguous or spurious relationships between terms. Failures due to the indexing subsystem were caused either by indexer error (omission or the use of inappropriate terms) or by a policy decision governing the number of terms assigned to an article. The most significant factor contributing to searching failures was found to be the searcher's failure to come up with the most effective query formulation. Failures due to inadequate interaction between the system and the requester resulted from discrepancy between stated and actual information needs because of a lack of opportunity for question negotiation between requester and search analyst.

On the basis of these findings the major recommendations of the study are the following:

1) Users' search request statements should be improved to describe search requirements more precisely.

2) The distinction between "depth" and "non-depth" journals should be abandoned and each article should be treated on its own merit.

3) Further development of the MEDLARS vocabulary should be based on continuous inputs from the indexing and search operations.

4) The use of sub-headings should be extended to increase the specificity of the vocabulary and to reduce the number of ambiguous term relationships.

5) The integration between the activities of indexing, searching and vocabulary control should be generally increased. [1]

References

1. Lancaster, Frederick W. "Evaluating the Performance of a Large Computerized Information System," Journal of the American Medical Association, 207:114-120, Jan. 6, 1969.

2. The Principles of MEDLARS. Bethesda, Maryland. National Library of Medicine, 1970. 77p. For sale by the Superintendent of Documents, U.S. Government Printing Office, Washington, D.C. (ED 043 336)

3. Stiller, Joy D. "Use of On-line Remote Access Information Retrieval Systems." In Proceedings of the American Society for Information Science, Vol. 7, 1970. pp. 107-109.

The MARC System

The MARC System was established as part of the automation program of the Library of Congress. The Library of Congress automation program has two major objectives: (1) determining methods by which its large scale internal operations can be performed more efficiently with the aid of computers, and (2) the development of standards for efficient and effective use of computers for exchange of bibliographic data among libraries.[1]

Mechanization of the bibliographic activities of the Library of Congress represents a type of system in which a machine record is created from manually organized information to be used (1) for the production of tools for manual searching, such as catalog cards and printed lists, and (2) for the mechanical searching of the machine file.

The machine records produced by the Library of Congress are intended both for its own use, and for use as input for local processing. The primary difference between the objectives of the MARC System and those of MEDLARS is the great emphasis of the former on facilitating the decentralized production of catalog cards or bibliographic listings from centrally produced machine-readable records. While the implications of this for planning at the local level need to be further clarified, there is no doubt that local agencies should make their own systems compatible with the machine-readable data that are available from the Library of Congress.

The MARC Pilot Project, which began in November 1966 and continued until June 1968, was intended to give an opportunity to libraries to experiment with the machine-readable data produced at the Library of Congress and to report back on their experiences. The primary concern was with the suitability of the data included in the records and the machine format of the records.

Experience in use and recommendations from the participants led to a revised format, the MARC II "communications format," and full-scale distribution service in the revised MARC II format began in March 1969. Libraries and other organizations subscribing to the service receive weekly tapes which presently contain cataloging information for English language monographs processed that week by the Library of Congress.

Since experience with MARC showed that the highest cost factor of record conversion relates to human editing (the assignment of tags and codes to the bibliographic record to define their content explicitly for machine processing) and to proofreading, a study was initiated by the Library of Congress to explore the feasibility of assigning tags and codes automatically by computer.[2]

The Library of Congress RECON Project (Retrospective Conversion Project) is concerned with the problems of large scale conversion of retrospective catalog records.[3]

The MARC II Record Format for Monographs

Each MARC record includes information corresponding to information normally found on a Library of Congress catalog card plus some additional data to facilitate machine processing. Records are stored sequentially on magnetic tape, constituting a direct file.

The format of a record refers to its structure, content and coding. The MARC II record for monographs is a variable length record made up of fixed fields and variable fields. A fixed field contains data which are always ex-

Representative Machine Applications 147

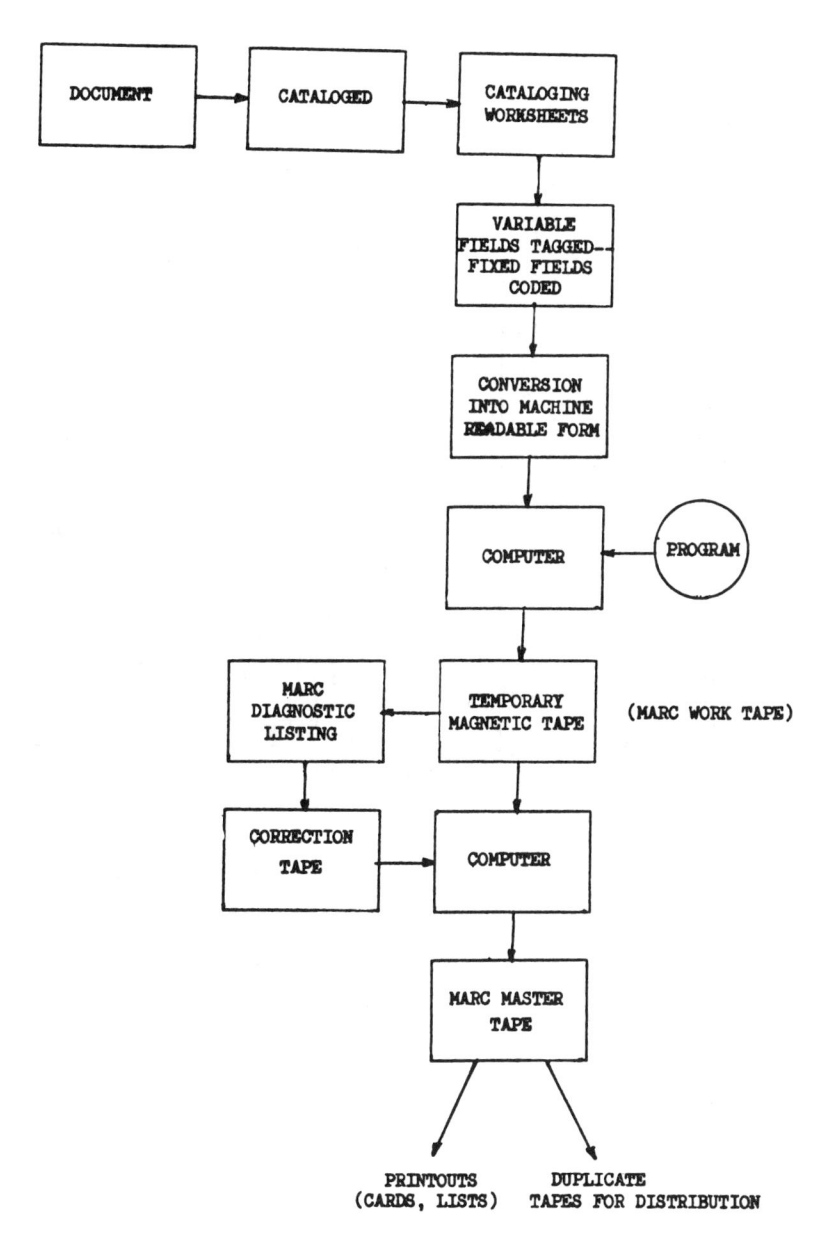

Figure 35. The MARC System

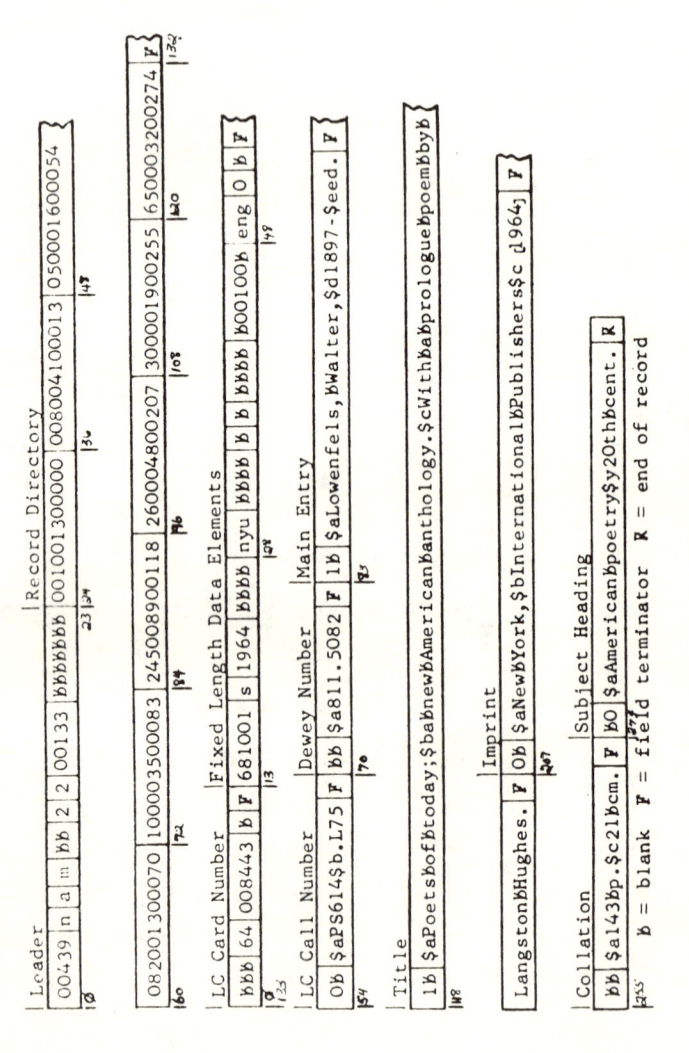

Figure 36. LC Card in MARC II Format

pressed by the same number of characters, and a variable field contains data the length of which varies from record to record. An example of the former is the date of publication which may always be expressed as four numeric characters |1|9|7|1| and an example of the latter is the title of a publication.

The MARC II record is made up of the following major parts:

Leader	Record Directory	Control Fields	Variable Fields

The <u>Leader</u> is of fixed length and contains 24 characters.

The <u>Record Directory</u> is made up of fixed length entries, 12 characters each. Each 12 character entry corresponds to either a control field or a variable field in the record and contains its identification tag, its length, and its starting position.

The <u>Control Fields</u> contain alphanumeric data elements, many of which are of fixed length.

The <u>Variable Fields</u> are made up of variable length alphanumeric data. [4]

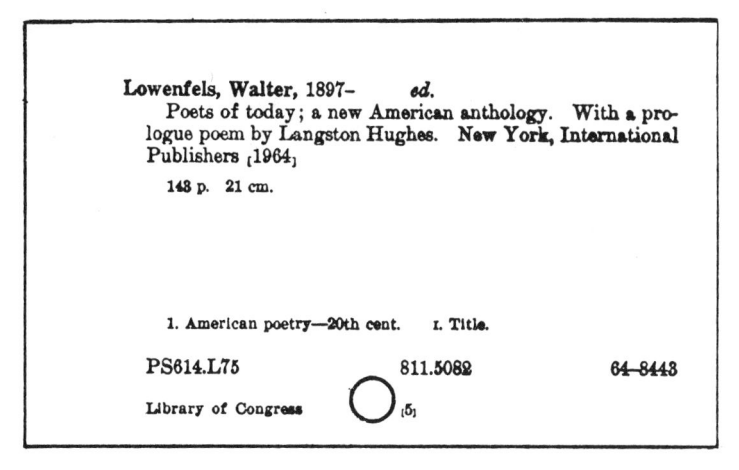

```
   Lowenfels, Walter, 1897-      ed.
      Poets of today; a new American anthology. With a pro-
   logue poem by Langston Hughes. New York, International
   Publishers [1964]
      148 p.  21 cm.


      1. American poetry—20th cent.    I. Title.
   PS614.L75                  811.5082              64-8443
      Library of Congress    ◯  [5]
```

Figure 36a. Library of Congress Card

The information contained in the Leader and the Record Directory is utilized when different fields and data elements in the record are accessed.

Since the first five characters of the Leader give you the logical record length and characters 12-16 give you the base address of the data, and since each Record Directory entry gives you the length and starting position of its corresponding field, it is easy to compute the starting position of each field from the beginning of the logical record.

For example, in Figure 36 the logical record length is 439 characters and the base address of the data is 133. If we wish to compute the character position in which the Title Field begins, we have to locate the Record Directory entry for the Title Field, the code for which is 245. In our example this is the sixth entry in the Record Directory. This entry also indicates that the Title Field is 89 characters long and that it begins in character position 118. Adding 118 + 132 = 250, which gives us the starting character position for the Title Field from the beginning of the logical record. Counting 89 characters, beginning with character 250, will get us to character position 338, which is the last character in the Title Field, the Field Terminator (F).

References

1. Reimers, Paul R. and Henriette D. Avram. "Automation and the Library of Congress: 1970," Datamation, 16:138-143, June 1970.

2. Format Recognition Process for MARC Records. A Logical Design. Chicago, American Library Association, 1970.

3. Avram, Henriette D., "The RECON Pilot Project: a Progress Report," Journal of Library Automation, 3:102-114, June 1970.

4. Library of Congress. MARC Manuals Used by the Library of Congress. Chicago, American Library Association, 1969.

PRODUCTION OF A FILE FOR MANUAL SEARCHING FROM MECHANICALLY ORGANIZED INFORMATION

General Diagram

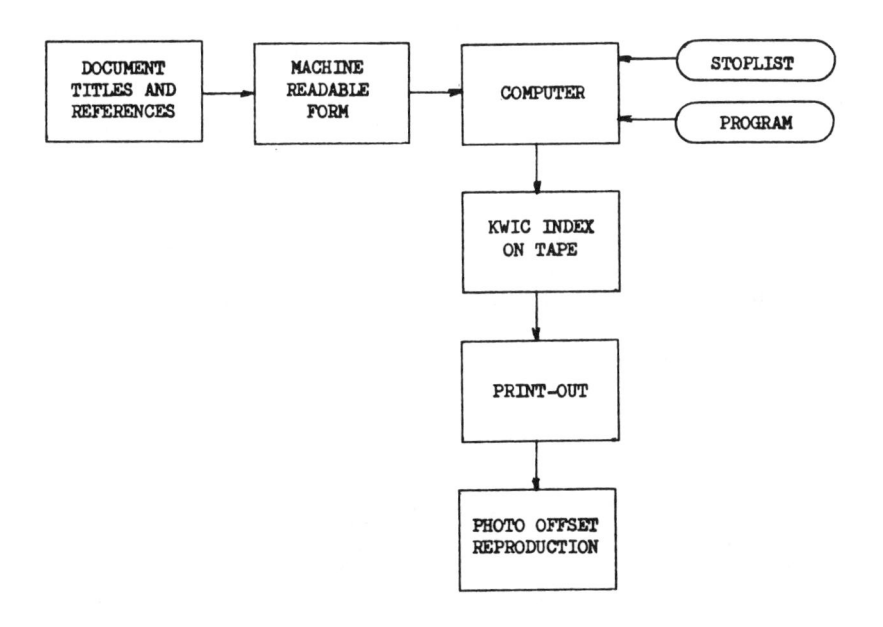

Figure 37.

Example: KWIC Index

The term "KWIC Index" has become a generic term in information science and technology referring to a variety of machine-produced permuted title indexes. As the diagram shows, this method is quite different from previously discussed computer applications because indexing is done by the computer rather than by human indexers, and the computer indexes words rather than concepts. The implications of content analysis based on words have been discussed in the section on word indexing and should be kept in mind in relation to KWIC indexes.

In its original form, as introduced by Hans Peter

Luhn in 1959, the KWIC index is an alphabetical list of keywords occurring in the titles to be indexed. The number of times each title is listed is the same as the number of keywords the title includes. The keywords are aligned on a particular column so that their alphabetic sequence can be observed readily. The listing of a keyword includes several words preceding and following it in the original title. How many other words can be shown depends on the total number of spaces allotted to the title on the print-out line. Keywords are established indirectly by having the machine reject all words contained in a predetermined list of non-significant words (stoplist); all remaining words then automatically become index terms. Words included in stoplists vary from index to index depending on which words are considered to lack meaning for indexing in a particular application. Each line in the index consists of three parts: the index word, the context, and the code referring to the complete bibliographic information about the document.

In addition to the KWIC index proper the index also includes a bibliography of items to which the user is referred through the reference code, as well as an alphabetical author listing of all the authors of all the documents appearing in the bibliography.

Separate machine-readable records for author, title, and source must be prepared in order to create the basic machine-readable records required for a KWIC index. Each record contains the reference code that was assigned to the particular document. The reference code may be assigned on the basis of document numbers, or according to an arbitrary numbering system, or it may be derived from the characteristics of the documents being indexed. The number of spaces allocated to each line in the KWIC index proper is usually a compromise between the amount of information desired, the physical size and cost of the publication, and the cost of the computer print-out mechanism. A 60-character index line is frequently used. This permits a two-column format on an 8-1/2" x 11" page if the print-out is reduced about 50 percent during offset reproduction. In some cases a 120-character line has been used in an effort to retain the full title.[1]

Figure 41 shows the steps involved in the preparation of the complete KWIC index.

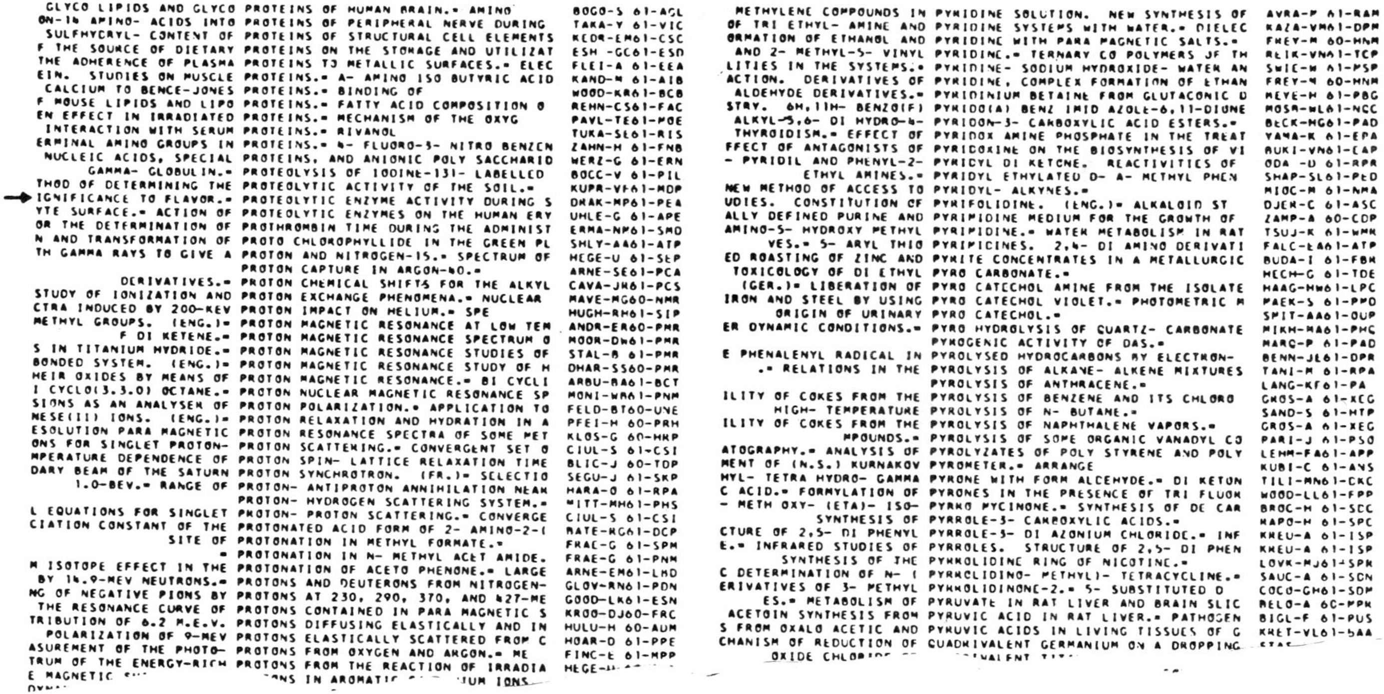

GLYCO LIPIDS AND GLYCO	PROTEINS OF HUMAN BRAIN.= AMINO	BOGO-S 61-AGL
ON-14 AMINO- ACIDS INTO	PROTEINS OF PERIPHERAL NERVE DURING	TAKA-Y 61-VIC
SULFHYDRYL- CONTENT OF	PROTEINS OF STRUCTURAL CELL ELEMENTS	KEDR-EM61-CSC
F THE SOURCE OF DIETARY	PROTEINS ON THE STORAGE AND UTILIZAT	ESH -GC61-ESD
THE ADHERENCE OF PLASMA	PROTEINS TO METALLIC SURFACES.= ELEC	FLEI-A 61-EEA
EIN. STUDIES ON MUSCLE	PROTEINS.= A- AMINO ISO BUTYRIC ACID	KAND-M 61-AIB
CALCIUM TO BENCE-JONES	PROTEINS.= BINDING OF	WOOD-KR61-BCB
F MOUSE LIPIDS AND LIPO	PROTEINS.= FATTY ACID COMPOSITION O	REHN-CS61-FAC
EN EFFECT IN IRRADIATED	PROTEINS.= MECHANISM OF THE OXYG	PAVL-TE61-MOE
INTERACTION WITH SERUM	PROTEINS.= RIVANOL	TUKA-SL61-RIS
ERMINAL AMINO GROUPS IN	PROTEINS.= 4- FLUORO-3- NITRO BENZEN	ZAHN-H 61-FNB
NUCLEIC ACIDS, SPECIAL	PROTEINS, AND ANIONIC POLY SACCHARID	WERZ-G 61-ERN
GAMMA- GLOBULIN.=	PROTEOLYSIS OF IODINE-131- LABELLED	BOCC-V 61-PIL
THOD OF DETERMINING THE	PROTEOLYTIC ACTIVITY OF THE SOIL.=	KUPR-VF61-MDP
→ IGNIFICANCE TO FLAVOR.=	PROTEOLYTIC ENZYME ACTIVITY DURING S	DRAK-MP61-PEA
YTE SURFACE.= ACTION OF	PROTEOLYTIC ENZYMES ON THE HUMAN ERY	UHLE-G 61-APE
OR THE DETERMINATION OF	PROTHROMBIN TIME DURING THE ADMINIST	ERMA-NM61-SMD
N AND TRANSFORMATION OF	PROTO CHLOROPHYLLIDE IN THE GREEN PL	SHLY-AA61-ATP
TH GAMMA RAYS TO GIVE A	PROTON AND NITROGEN-15.= SPECTRUM OF	HEGE-U 61-SEP
	PROTON CAPTURE IN ARGON-40.=	ARNE-SE61-PCA
DERIVATIVES.=	PROTON CHEMICAL SHIFTS FOR THE ALKYL	CAVA-JH61-PCS
STUDY OF IONIZATION AND	PROTON EXCHANGE PHENOMENA.= NUCLEAR	MAVE-MG60-NMR
CTRA INDUCED BY 200-KEV	PROTON IMPACT ON HELIUM.= SPE	HUGH-RH61-SIP
METHYL GROUPS. (ENG.)=	PROTON MAGNETIC RESONANCE AT LOW TEM	ANDR-ER60-PMR
F DI KETENE.=	PROTON MAGNETIC RESONANCE SPECTRUM O	MOOR-DW61-PMR
S IN TITANIUM HYDRIDE.=	PROTON MAGNETIC RESONANCE STUDIES OF	STAL-B 61-PMR
BONDED SYSTEM. (ENG.)=	PROTON MAGNETIC RESONANCE STUDY OF H	DHAR-SS60-PMR
HEIR OXIDES BY MEANS OF	PROTON MAGNETIC RESONANCE.= BI CYCLI	ARBU-BA61-BCT
I CYCLO(3.3.0) OCTANE.=	PROTON NUCLEAR MAGNETIC RESONANCE SP	MONI-WR61-PNM
SIONS AS AN ANALYSER OF	PROTON POLARIZATION.= APPLICATION TO	FELD-BT60-UNE
NESE(III) IONS. (ENG.)=	PROTON RELAXATION AND HYDRATION IN A	PFEI-H 60-PRH
ESOLUTION PARA MAGNETIC	PROTON RESONANCE SPECTRA OF SOME MET	KLOS-G 60-HRP
ONS FOR SINGLET PROTON-	PROTON SCATTERING.= CONVERGENT SET O	CIUL-S 61-CSI
MPERATURE DEPENDENCE OF	PROTON SPIN- LATTICE RELAXATION TIME	BLIC-J 60-TDP
DARY BEAM OF THE SATURN	PROTON SYNCHROTRON. (FR.)= SELECTIO	SEGU-J 61-SKP
1.0-BEV.= RANGE OF	PROTON- ANTIPROTON ANNIHILATION NEAR	HARA-O 61-RPA
	PROTON- HYDROGEN SCATTERING SYSTEM.=	MITT-MH61-PHS
L EQUATIONS FOR SINGLET	PROTON- PROTON SCATTERING.= CONVERGE	CIUL-S 61-CSI
CIATION CONSTANT OF THE	PROTONATED ACID FORM OF 2- AMINO-2-(	BATE-RG61-DCP
SITE OF	PROTONATION IN METHYL FORMATE.=	FRAC-G 61-SPM
=	PROTONATION IN N- METHYL ACET AMIDE.	FRAE-G 61-PNM
M ISOTOPE EFFECT IN THE	PROTONATION OF ACETO PHENONE.= LARGE	ARNE-EM61-LHD
BY 14.9-MEV NEUTRONS.=	PROTONS AND DEUTERONS FROM NITROGEN-	GLOV-RN61-PDN
NG OF NEGATIVE PIONS BY	PROTONS AT 230, 290, 370, AND 427-ME	GOOD-LK61-ESN
THE RESONANCE CURVE OF	PROTONS CONTAINED IN PARA MAGNETIC S	KROO-DJ60-FRC
TRIBUTION OF 6.2 M.E.V.	PROTONS DIFFUSING ELASTICALLY AND IN	HULU-H 60-ADM
POLARIZATION OF 9-MEV	PROTONS ELASTICALLY SCATTERED FROM C	HOAR-D 61-PPE
ASUREMENT OF THE PHOTO-	PROTONS FROM OXYGEN AND ARGON.= ME	FINC-E 61-MPP
TRUM OF THE ENERGY-RICH	PROTONS FROM THE REACTION OF IRRADIA	HEGE-U...
E MAGNETIC ...	...ONS IN AROMATIC ... IUM IONS	
DYN...		

METHYLENE COMPOUNDS IN	PYRIDINE SOLUTION. NEW SYNTHESIS OF	AVRA-P 61-RAM
OF TRI ETHYL- AMINE AND	PYRIDINE SYSTEMS WITH WATER.= DIELEC	KAZA-VM61-DPM
ORMATION OF ETHANOL AND	PYRIDINE WITH PARA MAGNETIC SALTS.=	FREY-M 60-HNM
AND 2- METHYL-5- VINYL	PYRIDINE.= TERNARY CO POLYMERS OF TH	REIK-VN61-TCP
LITIES IN THE SYSTEMS.=	PYRIDINE- SODIUM HYDROXIDE- WATER AN	SWIC-W 61-MSP
ACTION. DERIVATIVES OF	PYRIDINE, COMPLEX FORMATION OF ETHAN	FREY-M 60-HNM
ALDEHYDE DERIVATIVES.=	PYRIDINIUM BETAINE FROM GLUTACONIC D	MEYE-H 61-PBG
STRY. 6H,11H- BENZO(F)	PYRIDO(A) BENZ IMID AZOLE-6,11-DIONE	MOSA-WL61-NCC
ALKYL-5,6- DI HYDRO-4-	PYRIDON-3- CARBOXYLIC ACID ESTERS.=	BECK-HG61-PAD
THYROIDISM.= EFFECT OF	PYRIDOX AMINE PHOSPHATE IN THE TREAT	YAMA-K 61-EPA
FFECT OF ANTAGONISTS OF	PYRIDOXINE ON THE BIOSYNTHESIS OF VI	RUKI-VN61-CAP
- PYRIDIL AND PHENYL-2-	PYRIDYL DI KETONE. REACTIVITIES OF	ODA -U 61-RPR
ETHYL AMINES.=	PYRIDYL ETHYLATED O- A- METHYL PHEN	SHAP-SL61-PED
NEW METHOD OF ACCESS TO	PYRIDYL- ALKYNES.=	MIOC-M 61-NMA
UDIES. CONSTITUTION OF	PYRIFOLIDINE. (ENG.)= ALKALOID ST	DJER-C 61-ASC
ALLY DEFINED PURINE AND	PYRIMIDINE MEDIUM FOR THE GROWTH OF	ZAMP-A 60-CDP
AMINO-5- HYDROXY METHYL	PYRIMIDINE.= WATER METABOLISM IN RAT	TSUJ-K 61-WMR
VES.= 5- ARYL THIO	PYRIMICINES. 2,4- DI AMINO DERIVATI	FALC-EA61-ATP
ED ROASTING OF ZINC AND	PYRITE CONCENTRATES IN A METALLURGIC	BUDA-I 61-FBR
TOXICOLOGY OF DI ETHYL	PYRO CARBONATE.=	HECH-G 61-TDE
(GER.)= LIBERATION OF	PYRO CATECHOL AMINE FROM THE ISOLATE	HAAG-HW61-LPC
IRON AND STEEL BY USING	PYRO CATECHOL VIOLET.= PHOTOMETRIC M	PAEK-S 61-PMD
ORIGIN OF URINARY	PYRO CATECHOL.=	SPIT-AA61-OUP
ER DYNAMIC CONDITIONS.=	PYRO HYDROLYSIS OF QUARTZ- CARBONATE	MIKH-MA61-PHC
	PYROGENIC ACTIVITY OF DAS.=	MARQ-P 61-PAD
E PHENALENYL RADICAL IN	PYROLYSED HYDROCARBONS BY ELECTRON-	BENN-JE61-DPR
.= RELATIONS IN THE	PYROLYSIS OF ALKANE- ALKENE MIXTURES	TANI-M 61-RPA
	PYROLYSIS OF ANTHRACENE.=	LANG-KF61-PA
ILITY OF COKES FROM THE	PYROLYSIS OF BENZENE AND ITS CHLORO	GROS-A 61-XEG
HIGH- TEMPERATURE	PYROLYSIS OF N- BUTANE.=	SAND-S 61-HTP
ILITY OF COKES FROM THE	PYROLYSIS OF NAPHTHALENE VAPORS.=	GROS-A 61-XEG
MPOUNDS.=	PYROLYSIS OF SOME ORGANIC VANADYL CO	PARI-J 61-PSO
ATOGRAPHY.= ANALYSIS OF	PYROLYZATES OF POLY STYRENE AND POLY	LEHM-FA61-APP
MENT OF (N.S.) KURNAKOV	PYROMETER.= ARRANGE	KUBI-C 61-ANS
HYL- TETRA HYDRO- GAMMA	PYRONE WITH FORM ALDEHYDE.= DI KETON	TILI-MN61-DKC
C ACID.= FORMYLATION OF	PYRONES IN THE PRESENCE OF TRI FLUOR	WOOD-LL61-FPP
- METH OXY- (ETA)- ISO-	PYRRO MYCINONE.= SYNTHESIS OF DE CAR	BROC-H 61-SDC
SYNTHESIS OF	PYRROLE-3- CARBOXYLIC ACIDS.=	HAPO-H 61-SPC
CTURE OF 2,5- DI PHENYL	PYRROLE-3- DI AZONIUM CHLORIDE.= INF	KREU-A 61-ISP
E.= INFRARED STUDIES OF	PYRROLES. STRUCTURE OF 2,5- DI PHEN	KREU-A 61-ISP
SYNTHESIS OF THE	PYRROLIDINE RING OF NICOTINE.=	LOVK-MJ61-SPR
C DETERMINATION OF N- (	PYRROLIDINO- METHYL)- TETRACYCLINE.=	SAUC-A 61-SDN
ERIVATIVES OF 3- METHYL	PYRROLIDINONE-2.= 5- SUBSTITUTED D	COCO-GH61-SDM
ES.= METABOLISM OF	PYRUVATE IN RAT LIVER AND BRAIN SLIC	RELO-A 60-MPR
ACETOIN SYNTHESIS FROM	PYRUVIC ACID IN RAT LIVER.= PATHOGEN	BIGL-F 61-PUS
S FROM OXALO ACETIC AND	PYRUVIC ACIDS IN LIVING TISSUES OF G	KRET-VL61-SAA
CHANISM OF REDUCTION OF	QUADRIVALENT GERMANIUM ON A DROPPING	STAE...
OXIDE CHLORI...	...IVALENT TIT...	

Figure 38. Typical Page from a KWIC Index
(Arrow points to document which will be used in subsequent figures.)

```
       NUCLEIC ACIDS, SPECIAL PROTEINS, AND ANIONIC POLY SACCHARID    WERZ-G 61-ERN
             GAMMA- GLOBULIN.= PROTEOLYSIS OF IODINE-131- LABELLED    BOCC-V 61-PIL
     THOD OF DETERMINING THE PROTEOLYTIC ACTIVITY OF THE SOIL.=       KUPR-VF61-MDP
      IGNIFICANCE TO FLAVOR.= PROTEOLYTIC ENZYME ACTIVITY DURING S    DRAK-MP61-PEA
             YTE SURFACE.= ACTION OF PROTEOLYTIC ENZYMES ON THE HUMAN ERY  UHLE-G 61-APE
     OR THE DETERMINATION OF PROTHROMBIN TIME DURING THE ADMINIST     ERMA-NM61-SMD
```

```
     TEREOCHEMICAL COURSE OF ENZYMATIC STEROID 1, 2- DE HYDROGENA     HAYA-M 61-SCE
                   NZYMES.= ENZYMATIC SYNTHESIS OF COBAMIDE CO E      BRAD-R061-ESC
         TO FLAVOR.= PROTEOLYTIC ENZYME ACTIVITY DURING STORAGE OF RA DRAK-MP61-PEA
     RADIATION ON GROWTH AND ENZYME ACTIVITY OF ASPERGILLUS-ORYZA     FIEL-ML61-EIG
     ESISTANCE IN BACTERIA.  ENZYME FOR CONJUGATION OF P- AMINO-      AKIB-T 61-MTD
     DOSE PRODUCTION WITH AN ENZYME FROM THE MOLD POLYPORUS-CIRCI     AVIG-G 61-GDA
```

```
        SOLUTIONS AT 25-DEGS.= ACTIVITY COEFFICIENTS OF SODIUM CHLO   ROBI-RA61-ACS
     MISTRY AND POSSESSED OF ACTIVITY CONSIDERED AS PLASMINOGEN.=     SAND-G 61-IBG
           ANTIBIOTICS.= MONOMYCIN ACTIVITY DETERMINATION BY DIFFUSION IVAN-LP61-MAD
             OR.= PROTEOLYTIC ENZYME ACTIVITY DURING STORAGE OF RADIATION DRAK-MP61-PEA
     NG ENERGY ON PEROXIDASE ACTIVITY IN GREEN BEANS.= COMPLEMENT     BAKE-RW61-CET
```

```
     TOGRAPHY WITH WEAK BETA RADIATION.= RADIO CHROMA                 SCHA-HW61-RCW
     ETABOLISM COMPARED WITH RADIATION-INDUCED DISEASE.= ACTION O     KOLO-J 61-AMS
     IVITY DURING STORAGE OF RADIATION-STABILIZED RAW BEEF AND IT     DRAK-MP61-PEA
     ENE BY DENSELY IONIZING RADIATIONS.= RADIOLYSIS OF BENZ          GAEU-T 61-RBD
       - POSITRON SCATTERING.= RADIATIVE CORRECTIONS TO ELECTRON- E   FURL-G 61-RCE
             NATURE OF PER OXIDE- RADICAL CONDENSATES.=               NEKR-LI61-NPO
```

```
     RGICAL WORK.= FLUIDISED BED ROASTING OF ZINC AND PYRITE CONC     BUDA-I 61-FBR
     DENCE TIME IN FLUIDIZED BEDS.= GAS RESI                          HUNT-AR61-GRT
     ADIATION-STABILIZED RAW BEEF AND ITS SIGNIFICANCE TO FLAVOR.     DRAK-MP61-PEA
     BLE NITROGEN CONTENT OF BEEF AS INFLUENCED BY PRE- IRRADIATI     BAUT-FR61-CAN
     C RATINGS OF IRRADIATED BEEF DURING STORAGE.= EFFECT OF ADDE     WEST-RG61-EAE
     ENCES IN COMPOSITION OF BEEF LONGISSIMUS-DORSI MUSCLES DETER     LAWR-RA61-MMA
     CHEMICAL COMPOSITION OF BEEF PROTEIN FRACTIONS BEFORE AND AF     HEDI-PA61-CCB
```

```
     APHY.= DETERMINATION OF FLAVONOID COMPOUNDS AFTER THEIR PART     DAVI-J 61-DFC
     OLIDAGO-VIRGA-AUREA-L.= FLAVONOIDS IN THE HERB OF. GOLDENROD     SKRZ-L 61-FHG
     OMPOSITION OF SUNSTRUCK FLAVOR SUBSTANCE OF BEER.= C             KURO-Y 61-CSF
         AND ITS SIGNIFICANCE TO FLAVOR.= PROTEOLYTIC ENZYME ACTIVITY DRAK-MP61-PEA
     TESTING ROTOGRAVURE AND FLEXOGRAPHIC INKS.= USE OF STORMER V     CUMM-R 61-USV
     TER USING A RADIOACTIVE FLOAT.= RECORDING FLOW ME                TIMS-DW61-RFM
```

Figure 39

```
DRAI-LE60-NMR   DRAIN LE
                NUCLEAR MAGNETIC RESONANCE IN VANADIUM ALLOYS.=
                ARCH. SCI. (GENEVA), 1960, 13, SPECIAL NUMBER, 425-31.
DRAK-MP61-PEA   DRAKE MP            GERNON GD               KRAUS FJ
                PROTEOLYTIC ENZYME ACTIVITY DURING STORAGE OF
                RADIATION-STABILIZED RAW BEEF AND ITS SIGNIFICANCE
                TO FLAVOR.=
                J. FOOD SCI., 1961, 26, 156-62.
DREF-G 61-ACA   DREFAHL G           HUNECK S
                AMINO COMPOUNDS FROM ALPHA- AND BETA- BOSWELLIC ACID AND
                URSOLIC ACID.=
                CHEM. BER., 1961, 94, 1145-51.
DREF-G 61-CCA   DREFAHL G           HEUBLEIN G
                CYCLIC CONFIGURATION 1,2- AMINO ALCOHOLS. A CYCLIC
                CONFIGURATION 1,2- AMINO ALCOHOLS.=
                CHEM. BER., 1961, 94, 915-28.
DREF-G 61-SWR   DREFAHL G           PLOETNER G
                STILBENE. WITTIG REACTION WITH PARA- HALO- METHYL- BENZ
                ALDEHYDE.=
                CHEM. BER., 1961, 94, 907-14.
DREI-H 60-MSB   DREIZLER H          MAIER W                 RUDOLPH HD
                MICROWAVE SPECTROGRAPH WITH BACKWARD-WAVE OSCILLATORS AS
                RADIATION SOURCES. MICROWAVE SPECTRUM, STRUCTURE AND
                HINDERED INTERNAL ROTATION OF DI METHYL SULFIDE. (ENG.)=
                ARCH. SCI. (GENEVA), 1960, 13, SPECIAL NUMBER, 137.
DREL-H 61-RPA   DRELA H
                RECUPERATION OF PHTHALIC AHYDRIDE FROM THE DISTILLATION
                RESIDUE.=
                PRZEMYSL CHEM., 1961, 40, 6-8.
```

Figure 39 continued

156   Computers in Information Science

```
DRAI-LEBO-NMR   DRAIN LE
                  NUCLEAR MAGNETIC RESONANCE IN VANADIUM ALLOYS.-
                  ARCH. SCI. (GENEVA), 1960, 13, SPECIAL NUMBER, 425-31.
DRAK-MP61-PEA   DRAKE MP                     GERNON GO      KRAUS FJ
                  PROTEOLYTIC ENZYME ACTIVITY DURING STORAGE OF
                  RADIATION-STABILIZED RAW BEEF AND ITS SIGNIFICANCE
                  TO FLAVOR.-
                  J. FOOD SCI., 1961, 26, 156-62.
DREF-G 61-ACA   DREFAHL G                    HUNECK S
                  AMINO COMPOUNDS FROM ALPHA- AND BETA- BOSWELLIC ACID AND
                  URSOLIC ACID.-
                  CHEM. BER., 1961, 94, 1145-51.
DREF-G 61-CCA   DREFAHL G                    HEUBLEIN G
                  CYCLIC CONFIGURATION 1,2- AMINO ALCOHOLS.  A CYCLIC
                  CONFIGURATION 1,2- AMINO ALCOHOLS.-
                  CHEM. BER., 1961, 94, 915-28.
DREF-G 61-SMR   DREFAHL G                    PLOETNER G
                  STILBENE.  WITTIG REACTION WITH PARA- MALO- METHYL- BENZ
                  ALDEHYDE.-
                  CHEM. BER., 1961, 94, 907-14.
DREI-M 60-MSB   DREICLER M                   RUDOLPH HD
                  MICROWAVE SPECTROGRAPH WITH BACKWARD-WAVE OSCILLATORS AS
                  RADIATION SOURCES.  MICROWAVE SPECTRUM, STRUCTURE AND
                  HINDERED INTERNAL ROTATION OF DI METHYL SULFIDE.  (ENG.)-
                  ARCH. SCI. (GENEVA), 1960, 13, SPECIAL NUMBER, 137.
DMEL-M 61-RPA   DRELA M
                  RECUPERATION OF PHTHALIC ANHYDRIDE FROM THE DISTILLATION
                  RESIDUE.-
                  PRZEMYSL CHEM., 1961, 40, 6-8.
DRES-FK61-IGT   DRESCHER-KADEN FK            DITTMANN J
                  INTER GRANULAR TRANSPORT PROCESSES.-
                  NATURWISSENSCHAFTEN, 1961, 48, 217.
DRES-FK61-ODS   DRESCHER-KADEN FK
                  ORIGIN OF THE DARK SPHEROIDS OF ADAMELLO IONALITES.-
                  NATURWISSENSCHAFTEN, 1961, 48, 217.
DROZ-DV  -RBU   DROZDOV NS                   MATERANSKAIA NP
                  RELATIONSHIP BETWEEN THE UNSATURATED CONDITION AND THE AUTO
                  OXIDATION RATE IN MIXTURES OF TRI GLYCERIDES DERIVED
                  FROM NATURAL FATS.-
                  DOKLADY AKAD. NAUK S.S.S.R., 1961, 137, 602-5.
DROZ-VF61-EAC   DROZDOVSKII VF               LAVROVA TV      SOKOLOV SA
                  EFFECT OF ANHYDRIDES OF CARBOXYLIC ACIDS ON REGENERATION
                  OF RUBBER.-
                  KAUCHUK I REZINA, 1961, 20, NO. 3, 33-5.
DRUC-M 61-PSC   DRUCKERY H                   PREUSSMANN R    SCHMAEHL D
                  MUELLER M
                  PRODUCTION OF STOMACH CANCER IN THE RAT BY MEANS OF NITROS
                  AMIDE.-
                  NATURWISSENSCHAFTEN, 1961, 48, 165.
DUBI-MM61-APS   ...                          VISHNU...       ZAVERINA...
```

```
DYER-E 61-GID   DYER E                       SHYLUK S
                  GLYCYL IMINO DI- ACETIC ACID.-
                  J. ORG. CHEM., 1961, 26, 1321-2.
DYKM-R 61-FMD   DYKMAN R                     KRAUS FJ
                  FLUID MIXER DESIGN SPECIFICATIONS.-
                  CHEM. ENG. PROGR., 1961, 57, 122-31.
DYMO-TN61-PMH   DYMOVA TN                    STERLYADKINA ZK   SAFRONOV V
                  PREPARATION OF MAGNESIUM HYDRIDE.-
                  ZHUR. NEORG. KHIM., 1961, 6, NO. 4, 763-7.
DYMO-TN61-PMH   DYMOVA TN                    STERLYADKINA ZK   ELISEEVA N
                  PROPERTIES OF MAGNESIUM HYDRIDE.-
                  ZHUR. NEORG. KHIM., 1961, 6, NO. 4, 768-73.
DYNA-R 61-ISA   DYNAKOWSKI R                 KUBALSKI J
                  INFLUENCE OF THE SULPHURIC ACID COMENTATION ON T
                  METHANOL DETERMINATION BY WIDMARK/S METHOD.-
                  ACTA POLON. PHARM., 1961, 18, 21-9.
EBER-KC61-EGD   EBERL KC                     ...
                  EVALUATION OF THE GILMAN-HAUBEIN DETERMINATION OF
                  LITHIUM.-
                  J. ORG. CHEM., 1961, 26, 1309.
ECKS-Z 61-ECP   ECKSTEIN Z                   ORLOWSKI J
                  EXAMINATION OF THE CATALYTIC PROCESS OF DE HYDRO
                  CHLORINATION OF INACTIVE HEXA CHLORO CYCLO HEXA
                  ISOMERS.-
                  PRZEMYSL CHEM., 1961, NO. 102-5.
ECKS-Z 61-IAF   ECKSTEIN Z                   PLENKIEWICZ J    BYRDY S
                  INFLUENCE OF AROMATICALLY-BOUND FLUORINE ON THE I
                  ACTIVITY OF 1,1-DI PHENYL-2- NITRO PROPANE.-
                  PRZEMYSL CHEM., 1961, NO. 26-9.
EDEL-LI61-PSD   EDEL/MAN LI                  SOMINSKII DS     KOPCHIKOV
                  PORE SIZE DISTRIBUTION IN CEMENT ROCK.-
                  KOLLOID ZHUR., 1961, 23, 228-33.
EDGE-WR61-MVC   EDGELL WR                    SUMMITT R
                  HYDROGEN VIBRATIONS IN COBALT CARBONYL HYDRIDE.  I
                  CONSIDERATIONS.-
                  J. AM. CHEM. SOC., 1961, 83, 1772.
EFIM-EA61-ASG   EFIMOV EA                    ERUSALIMCHIK IG
                  ANODIC SOLUTION OF GERMANIUM IN THE PRESENCE OF RI
                  AGENTS.-
                  ZHUR. FIZ. KHIM., 1961, 35, 543-7.
EFIM-OM61-PAA   EFIMENKO OM                  MELNIKOVA TA     ZOZULYA RI
                  POLYPORENIC ACID-A - AN ANTIBIOTIC ISOLATED FROM
                  TINDER FUNGUS POLYPORUS-BETULINUS-(BULL)-KARST.
                  ANTIBIOTIKI, 1961, 6, 215-20.
EFRE-VP61-PN    EFREMENKO VP
                  A PROMISING NEMATOCIDE.-
                  ZASHCHITA RASTENII OT...
```

Figure 40. KWIC Bibliography Page

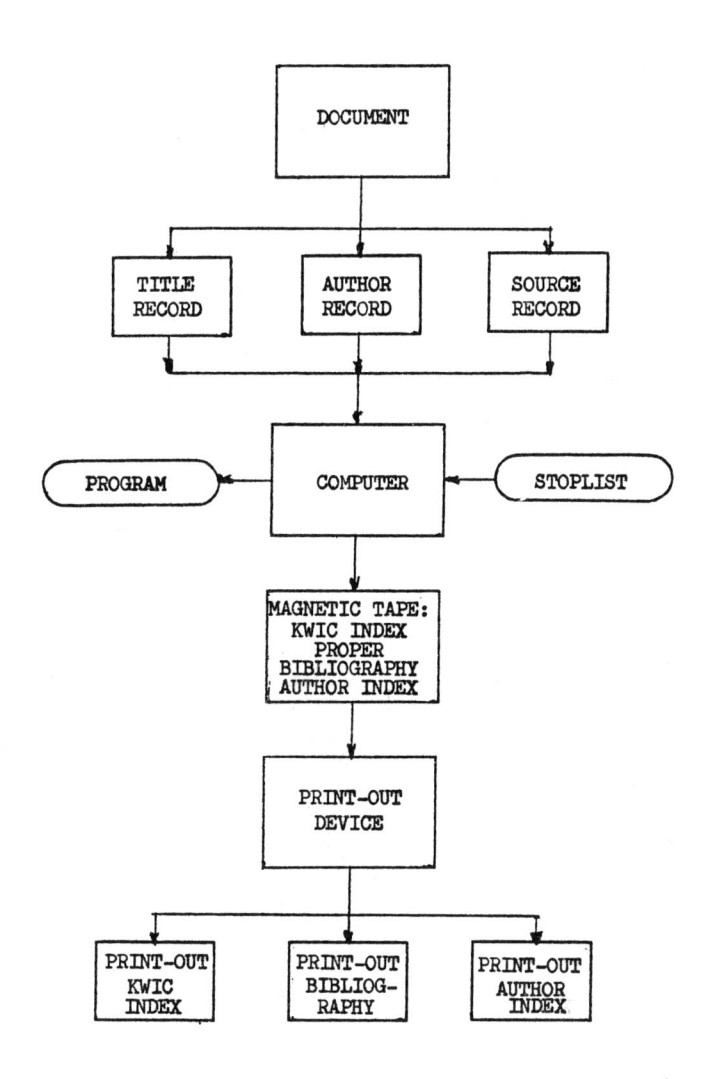

Figure 41. Steps Involved in the Preparation of the Complete KWIC Index

Multiple copies are produced from the printouts usually by photo offset, using an appropriate reduction ratio. Depending on the equipment which is available printouts will be in all capital letters or in capital and lower-case. The use of upper- and lower-case letters improves the legibility of the index but it does increase somewhat the cost of production.

The changes and developments which have occurred in the KWIC index concept since its introduction by Luhn relate both to its physical form and to its intellectual content. Some changes are concerned with the manipulation of the index line. In the KWOC (Key-Word-Out-of-Context) index, keywords are taken out of context and followed by the full title. WADEX (Word and Author Index) is a combination of subject and author entries; it treats the names of authors as keywords, thus combining the author index with the subject index.[2]

One of the problems related to the physical form of KWIC indexes has been their poor legibility resulting from high reduction ratios and the use of capital letters only. Problems related to the intellectual content of KWIC indexes relate to lack of vocabulary control and the frequently uninformative nature of document titles.[3] Problems concerning synonyms and variations in word usage and spelling were recognized in Luhn's first report. He, however, assumed that the expert in his field is sufficiently familiar with such variations to overcome this problem and that cross references could be used to take care of less obvious instances.[4] To improve the usefulness of titles for indexing, authors have been encouraged to write titles containing words useful for indexing. Rewriting of titles prior to machine processing has also been suggested. It should be noted, however, that such rewriting changes the original KWIC concept of automatic indexing and replaces it with a system in which manual indexing precedes machine processing.

Luhn envisaged the KWIC index as a current awareness tool of temporary value which was to be superseded by a more powerful intellectual tool. This is how Chemical Titles has been used in the Chemical Abstracts system. Adequacy of the KWIC index as a retrospective tool is questionable. It has been adopted as such, primarily because the production of cumulative indexes is simple and the method is considered to be relatively inexpensive, although there is very little cost information available.

So far as the function of the KWIC concept is concerned, there is good reason to believe that this approach has reached the limit of its capability. We seem to have come full cycle since Luhn's original idea and have reached a point at which some of the variations suggested are so elaborate that they defeat the simplicity and usefulness of the original approach, and result in little more than rather inadequate, not automatic, and not necessarily inexpensive indexing.

References

1. International Business Machines Corporation. Key-Word-In-Context (KWIC) Indexing. White Plains, N.Y., 1962. 21p. (E20-8091-0)

2. Fischer, Margaret. "The KWIC Concept: A Retrospective View," American Documentation, 17:57-70, April 1966.

3. Lewis, Robert F. "KWIC--Is It Quick?" Bulletin of the Medical Library Association, pp. 142-147, Jan. 1964.

4. Luhn, Hans Peter. Key-Word-In-Context Index for Technical Literature. (KWIC Index) RC-127. IBM Corporation, Yorktown Heights, N.Y., 1959.

MECHANICAL MATCHING OF MANUALLY CREATED INTEREST PROFILES WITH MANUALLY CREATED DOCUMENT SURROGATES

General Diagram

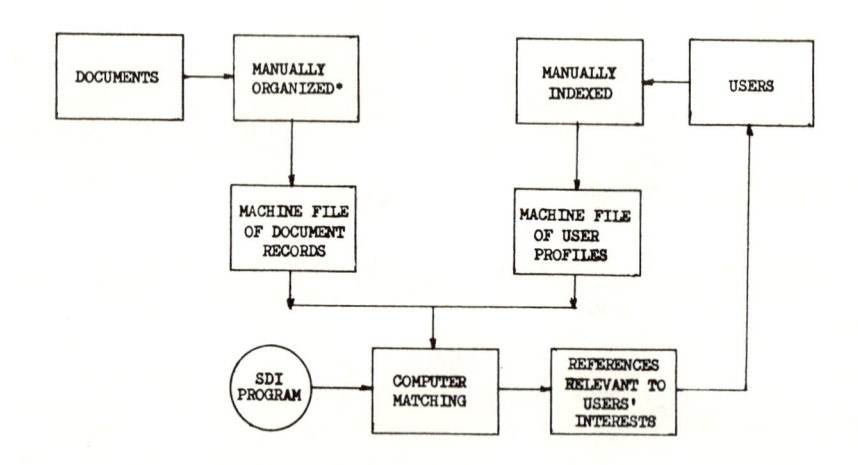

Figure 42

Example: Selective Dissemination of Information (SDI)

Stated in the most general way, Selective Dissemination of Information (SDI)[1] consists of the mechanical matching of manually created document surrogates with manually created interest profiles. The method, originated by Luhn,[2] mechanizes a service which has been performed for a long time in special libraries on a manual basis, simply by drawing the attention of individuals to materials that relate to their particular interests. Selective Dissemination of Information systems are based on two major pieces of information:

1) Who is interested in what; and
2) What the documents in the system are about.

On the basis of these two major pieces of information the system performs the following processes:

lary control, and the intellectual problems involved are essentially the same as those in searching a system with no vocabulary control. The implications of uncontrolled vocabularies were discussed in detail in the section on word indexing.

Profiles in systems that are based on natural language tend to include a larger number of terms than are required in a system with a controlled vocabulary because they must include all possible synonyms for the words that relate to the users' interests. To cut down on the number of profile terms, truncated terms or word stems, to stand for several complete terms, have been used. This practice can result in both the lowering of precision and the lowering of recall, depending on the characteristics of the particular stemming algorithm used. (See more on this in the unit on Project Intrex.)

A number of SDI systems use weights to indicate the relative importance of a term in the user's profile, in an attempt to achieve a high precision ratio and, possibly, reduce the quantity of the output sent to the user. However, there is no evidence that a high precision ratio is a generally desirable objective. High recall ratios may be preferred when completeness of coverage is important or when the system as a whole contains relatively little material of potential interest to the user.

Updating of user profiles is an important problem. As changes occur in users' interests, irrelevant terms in their profiles must be replaced with those describing their current interests. Some systems have built-in feedback mechanisms to let the manager of the system know that adjustment is required. Other systems leave it to the users to initiate changes in their profiles.

A "response" card is frequently used as a feedback mechanism. This card is attached to the information-card-- the card describing the document selected for him by the system--that is sent to the user. After examining the information card, the user is also asked to indicate such things as whether or not the document was relevant to his needs or whether or not he has seen it before. If he wishes to see the document the user also indicates that on the response card. This type of information is then fed back into the system so that its effectiveness can be assessed and adjustments made by adjusting the user's profile either to meet any

--Matching descriptions of users' information requirements against the descriptions of contents of documents;

--Selection of documents whose description matches the users' information requirements;

--Distribution of information about selected documents;

--Distribution of the documents themselves;

--Modification of user profiles on the basis of feedback from the system or from the users.[3]

User Profiles

Descriptions of users' information requirements are normally referred to as _user profiles_. Creation of a profile involves finding out through questioning of individuals what their interests are and the expression of these interests in an index language that is compatible with the documentary store. For reasons of economy there has been some experimentation to replace individual profiles with _group profiles_. This approach is based on the assumption that it is possible to identify groups within an organization with sufficiently similar interests to permit dissemination of information to groups rather than to individuals. Currently an investigation is in progress that intends to explore the relative effectiveness of group profiles and of various methods of grouping.[4]

The need to make profiles compatible with the characteristics of the retrieval file may involve a number of different problems. When the file consists of documents indexed through the use of a controlled vocabulary the same controlled vocabulary must be used for the preparation of the profiles. This is true, of course, whether the system is based on an internally generated data base or whether it is centered around machine-readable products obtained from outside sources.

Profiles can be also matched against the natural language text of abstracts or the titles of documents, as is the case with data bases available from Chemical Abstracts and Psychological Abstracts, for example. The preparation of profiles then must take into account the absence of vocab

Representative Machine Applications 163

change in his interests or to alter the level of match when the user wishes to receive more or less information.

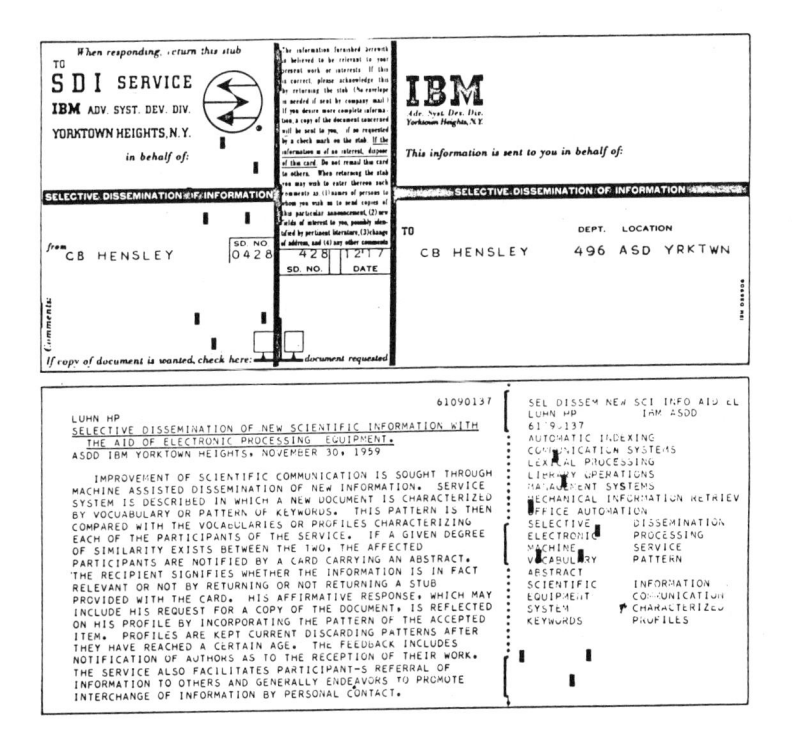

Figure 43. Notification Card, Printed Front and Back

Matching Strategies

From the mechanical point of view, matching is simple. Whenever there is a satisfactory match the computer selects the appropriate document. The complexities of matching relate to the adequate definition of "satisfactory match."

The definition of satisfactory match will be influenced by the combined effect of such variables as:

--The a priori (overall) match between document

content and user interests;

--The number of documents in the system;

--The optimum number of documents to be received by a given user over a given period of time;

--Whether the general objective is to be highly selective or fairly inclusive;

--The overall basis of the system, i.e. whether a controlled vocabulary is used or whether the system has no vocabulary control. In case of the former the characteristics of the index language used will influence the definition of satisfactory match.

Definitions of satisfactory match may range from the match of a single term in the document description and in the user profile to complex strategies involving Boolean functions and the calculation of threshold values on the basis of weights.

Boolean search strategy combines user profile terms in a Boolean function whose logical operators are AND, OR and NOT. Weights assigned to terms in user profiles can be summed algebraically and compared to a threshold value. If the figure equals or exceeds this value the document is selected. The sum of weights can be used as a relevance score to arrange documents according to their decreasing order of relevance; then the predetermined number of documents selected from the top of the list can be sent to the user. When running profiles against abstracts, the order of terms for a satisfactory match in the text can be stipulated, or it can be stipulated that two or more words must or must not appear within a sentence to be matched.

There are too many other possible approaches for complete listing here. However, it is easy to see that the definitions of satisfactory match present essentially the same problem that is involved in the formulation of the search strategy in a retrieval system. In one case we are matching user profiles against the documentary store, in the other we are matching queries against it. In both cases the mechanical problems are relatively simple and straightforward and the effectiveness of the system will hinge on the solution of the intellectual problems--those which were just discussed as well as many others which relate to subjects discussed earlier in the sections dealing with "Processing Documents for Input" and the "Retrieval of Documents."

This is a rather important point because people with only superficial familiarity with SDI systems commonly fail to look beyond the simple mechanics of computer matching.

Overall System Effectiveness

The importance of the efficient overall functioning of the total system cannot be overemphasized. This is essentially a management problem, to assure the speedy flow of information and materials between user and system.

The success of any user-oriented service will be ultimately determined by its value to the user. There is very little information available in the literature relating to the effectiveness of SDI systems, and studies are needed on this aspect of the problem. One such study, now in progress at the National Electronics Research Council in England,[5] is intended to determine the value of an SDI service to different classes of users and the extent to which the value may vary with the user's subject interests, his degree of specialization, the type of research he is doing, etc. On the basis of feedback from the user, the efficacy of the system is tested in terms of its provision of the required information and the extent to which it screens out irrelevant materials.

While there are few dependable cost figures published in the literature for SDI systems, it is generally agreed that the cost tends to be high. As the number of profiles goes up, the fixed costs are distributed over a larger number of units, and this results in a lower unit cost per profile. While it is assumed by some that the use of group profiles instead of individual profiles will result in a reduction of cost, little is known about the extent of the savings from the point of view of cost-effectiveness.

Multiple Data Bases

An interesting development which affects the cost of the operation of SDI systems is the use of multiple data bases within a given system. This expands the coverage of the SDI system and, at the same time, should reduce the unit cost per document covered. It is assumed that a reduction in cost should result from the acquisition of preprocessed data bases, as compared to in-house processing. However, there are no comparative cost figures available which would take into consideration, among other things, the duplication of coverage among the different data bases.

The use of multiple data bases by a single organization also raises the problem of intersystem compatibility and convertibility of vocabularies as well as the machine format of the various data bases involved. The manager of the SDI system has two choices here: to treat the different data bases separately or to merge them into a single one. The first approach implies that each data base must be searched separately for a given query, with the query re-formulated for each search to make it compatible with the particular data base being searched. The second approach requires the conversion of the vocabularies of the various data bases into a single one and the re-formatting of the various records into a common format. Difficulties relating to vocabulary conversion arise from differences in the subject interests of the vocabularies and differences in the terminological conventions employed by the various vocabularies. Studies relating to vocabulary conversion found that low convertibility can result from a lack of correspondence between the terms of the vocabularies or from a lack of interest on the part of one system in the documents in the collection of the other system. The solution of the problem depends to a considerable extent on the degree and quality of cross-referencing in the vocabularies; consequently, controlled vocabularies convert better than do uncontrolled vocabularies.[6]

References

1. Housman, Edward M., comp. A Survey of Current Systems for Selective Dissemination of Information (SDI). Washington, D.C., American Society for Information Science, 1969. 145p. (AD 692 792)

2. Luhn, Hans Peter. "Selective Dissemination of New Scientific Information With the Aid of Electronic Processing Equipment," American Documentation, 12:131-138, April 1961.

3. Bivona, William A., et al. Selective Dissemination

of Information: Review of Selected Systems and a Design for Army Technical Libraries. Reading, Mass., Information Dynamics Co., 1966. (AD 636 916)

4. Maloney, Ruth Kay. An Analysis of Group Profiling for SDI Systems in Industrial Communities. Ph.D. Thesis, Rutgers University (In progress.)

5. Aitchison, T. M., et al. "Developments Toward a Computer-Based Information Service in Physics, Electrotechnology and Control." Information Storage and Retrieval, 4:177-186, 1968.

6. Wall, Eugene and Herbert Landau. "Interconvertibility of Subject Vocabularies." In: Proceedings of the 7th Annual National Colloquium on Information Retrieval, May 8-9, 1970, Philadelphia, Pa. A. D. Berton, ed., Philadelphia, The College of Physicians of Philadelphia, 1970. pp. 103-111.

ON-LINE RETRIEVAL OF MANUALLY ORGANIZED INFORMATION

General Diagram

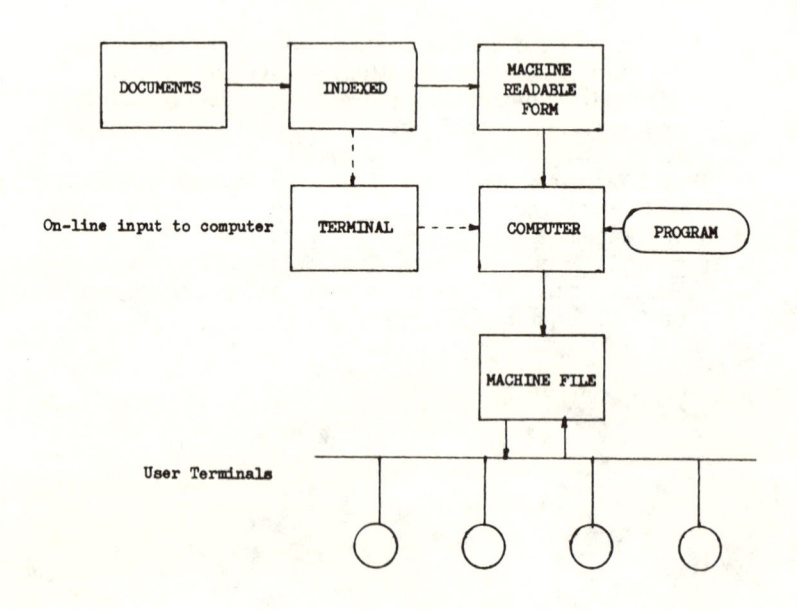

Figure 44

<u>Examples:</u> Project Intrex
MAC Technical Information Project

<u>Project Intrex</u>

Project Intrex[1] (<u>in</u>formation <u>t</u>ransfer <u>ex</u>periment), of which the Augmented Catalog Program is a part, is a program of research and experimentation established with the twofold objective of finding long term solutions for operational problems of large libraries and of developing competence in the field of information transfer engineering.

The research program is addressed to the broad problem of access; in particular, access to bibliographic materials, documents, and data-banks. The Project seeks to improve the efficiency of catalog searches by utilizing interactive computing techniques and by providing rapid access to full-text displays by utilizing microfilm storage and facsimile transmission. The core activities of the program focus on the following main areas: augmented catalog, full-text access, display consoles, and the model library project.

The Augmented Catalog Program

The Augmented Catalog experiment is based on a small collection of documents in the field of materials engineering. Augmentation refers to the increased coverage, depth, and manipulation available in the system as compared to conventional library catalogs. Increased coverage means the inclusion of all literature forms; increased depth provides for more access through more exhaustive indexing; and manipulation refers to the user's ability to have direct access to the computer file to perform searches for documents.

Indexing of documents is done by skilled human indexers, and their indexing decisions are recorded on worksheets. A very detailed instruction manual, concerning primarily the assignment of non-subject type of tags, was prepared.[2] The assignment of a large number of non-subject type of tags is intended to explore the types of descriptive information that will have the greatest value to the user. In subject indexing, "uncontrolled phrases" are used to describe the content of the document. These phrases are included in the document record along with all other information about the document. Documents entering the system are also microfiched as part of the Text Access Program.

At an earlier stage of the Project, records were keyed, off-line, onto punched paper tape. This method was changed in January 1971 to an on-line method of keyboarding index record data, using the IBM 2741 terminal. On-line inputting is followed by a correction loop, formatting, and merging of the new records into the data base.

While the complete document records are organized into a direct file the three most frequently used fields of the index record--author, title, and subject--are structured into two inverted files, one for authors' names and a second for subject and title terms.

The author inverted file is composed of lists of references, one such list for each unique author's last name. Each reference contains information related to an index record entry which has the particular author's last name in the author field.

The subject/title inverted file is composed of a collection of word stem lists. Each record in the file corresponds to a word stem and an associated list of references to those index records which contain any of the words in the title or subject field that correspond to the stem.

To be entered into the subject/title inverted file, uncontrolled indexing phrases and document titles go through a phrase decomposition process in which the common words are excluded and all others are stemmed. The stemming algorithm is designed to reduce semantically or morphologically related words (such as computing and computation) to a common stem (comput-).

Stemming is a frequently used technique to compensate for some of the problems inherent in the use of uncontrolled vocabularies. By grouping words together under a common stem it is possible to reduce the number of records in an inverted index file. The same method can be used to reduce the number of terms in a query or in an SDI profile.

Stemming obviously introduces some degree of uncertainty into the system and the performance of the system will be affected by the quality of the stemming algorithm. The two kinds of errors that can occur are overstemming, resulting in low precision, and understemming, which results in low recall.[3]

Searching the Data Base

The users' queries are entered into the computer via a console and are interpreted by a set of interface programs. The results of this interpretation are passed to the retrieval programs which do the actual processing from the data base. The results of the search are passed back through the interface programs and are presented to the user via a console.

Through the facilities provided by the time-sharing

Representative Machine Applications

system, several users can access the data base simultaneously through consoles in various remote locations.

Since initial access to the data base is through the inverted files, subject access must be through stems, which in turn means that the query must be subjected to the same decomposition and stemming procedure as the titles and indexing phrases.

Queries involving descriptive information other than subject and author are further processed by searching those records of the direct file that were isolated as a result of initial access to one of the inverted files.

Command Language

The Intrex command language has a rigid but simple formal syntax with natural language English words. Non-English words were dropped when users were found to have trouble learning them.

The command language is flexible in the sense that it allows for the abbreviation of commands and allows the user to switch to a "short" mode, which suppresses or shortens most of the instructional material presented in the computer responses.

Features of the command language that were found to cause the user troubles were such things as punctuation (users tend to be careless about it), the use of jargon words, and irregularities in the language. The fact that no user-originated command can hurt the system, and that the system recovers from most errors in such a way that the user can easily get going again, was found useful.

Text-Access Program

As part of the Text-Access Program the Intrex system provides for full text storage and retrieval. While the retrieval file of document surrogates is stored in digital form for computer searching, the full text of the corresponding Intrex document collection is stored on microfiche.

In searching the retrieval file the user interrogates the system by means of the typewriter keyboard of a remote terminal. The output of the system, a list of bibliographic references relevant to the user's query, is displayed on the terminal's cathode ray tube. In addition, the full-text of documents can also be displayed on the same CRT tube in response to the user's request. This type of system, in which the same terminal provides access to both the computer-stored index file and the microfilm-stored text, represents a highly sophisticated integration of the technologies of computer processing, microfilm storage, and facsimile transmission.

   Text-access is initiated in response to an "output text" command from the user. The computer looks up the document's microfiche address number, the buffer/controller changes from catalog to text-access mode, and the text request is automatically transmitted to the microfiche central store. When the text is displayed on the CRT tube, the terminal functions as an off-line display station. An appropriate message transmitted from the computer or a key actuated at the keyboard will cause the terminal to revert to a computer-user interactive mode.

   Permanent printed copies of the full text of articles are available from a separate reproduction station. Methods of providing hard copy directly from the CRT displays are currently being implemented.

MAC Technical Information Project

   The overall design objectives of the MAC Technical Information System (TIP) at MIT and Project Intrex are similar in that they both provide for retrieval of information on-line from a time-shared computer through user-controlled remote terminals. Differences between the two systems concern such things as the characteristics of the data base, file organization, and hardware configuration.

   The MAC/TIP System uses standard teletype terminals instead of the cathode ray tube terminals which have been developed in Project Intrex. In the MAC System the user types in his question and receives the response printed back by the same typewriter, rather than having it displayed in front of him on a cathode ray tube. The user interacts with the system by means of a language very close to natur-

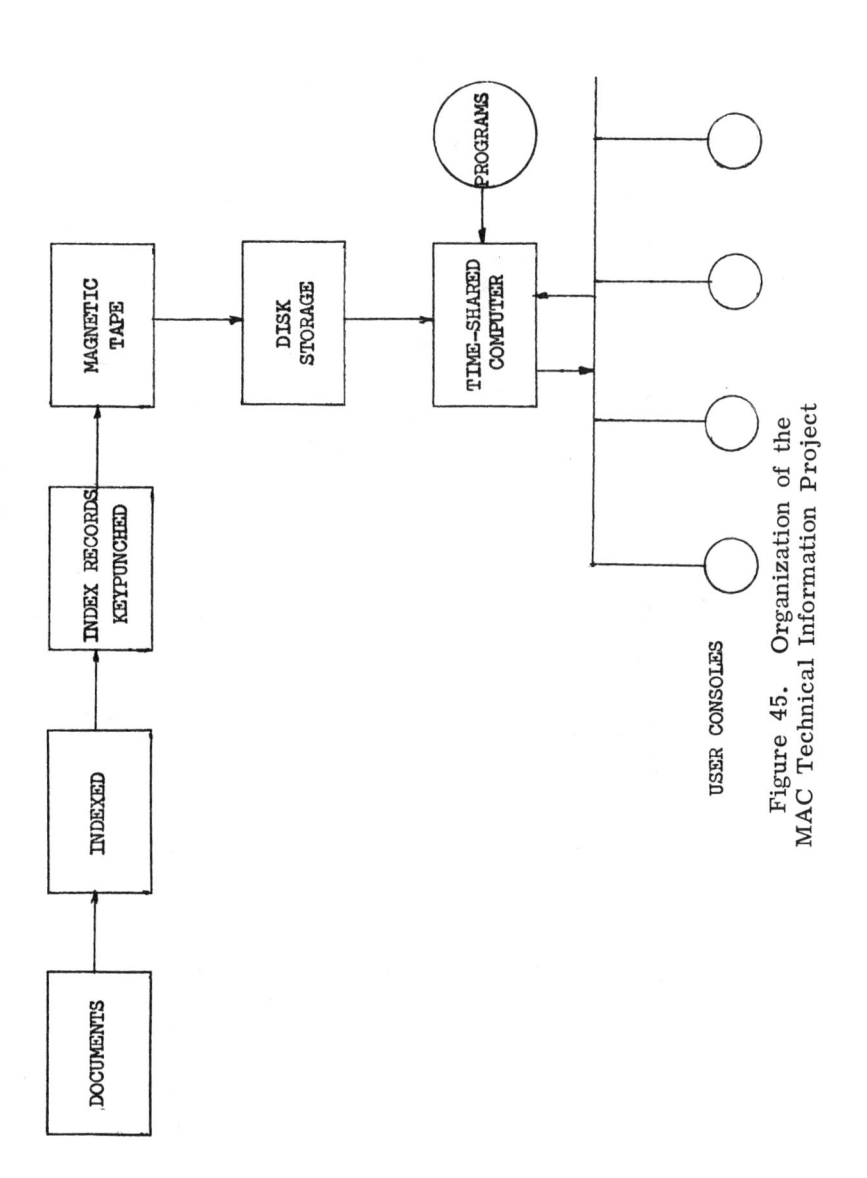

Figure 45. Organization of the MAC Technical Information Project

al English. In the Technical Information Project the language of the user includes such simple instructions as:

> SEARCH:ALL--means search the entire store;
>
> SEARCH:ALL-NEW--means the last volume of each journal;
>
> SEARCH, in combination with a journal title, will search that journal only;
>
> FIND, in combination with an author's name, will retrieve all documents by the particular author;
>
> OUTPUT command selects one of several options available for output such as PRINT, COUNT, STORE. [5,6]

References

1. Project Intrex Semiannual Activity Reports. Cambridge, Mass., Massachusetts Institute of Technology. 1965-

2. Benenfeld, Alan R., E. J. Gurley, and J. E. Rust. Cataloging Manual. ESL-TM-303. Cambridge, Mass., Massachusetts Institute of Technology, 1967.

3. Lovins, Julie B. "Error evaluation of stemming algorithms as clustering-algorithms," Journal of the American Society for Information Science, 22:28-40, January-February 1971.

4. Kusik, Robert L. A File Organization for the Intrex Information Retrieval System on the 360/67 CP/CMS Time-Sharing System. Cambridge, Mass., Massachusetts Institute of Technology, 1970. (ESL-TM-415)

5. Kessler, M. M. "The MIT Technical Information Project," Physics Today, 18:28-36, March 1965.

6. Kessler, M. M. TIP System Report. Technical Information Program. Cambridge, Mass., Massachusetts Institute of Technology, Oct. 1967.

PRODUCTION OF PRINTED INDEXES

The production of printed indexes and catalogs is an important area of computer application.

Until fairly recently in the production of these tools the use of the computer was limited to two main functions:

1) The arrangement of records according to different sort-keys in various sequences; and

2) The updating of the file, through additions and deletions, for the production of cumulated editions.

The computer has also been used for such purposes as to validate terms and to perform some limited editing functions.

As a result of advances in computer typesetting, the use of the computer was greatly extended to include the production of tape output which can be used to activate high speed typesetting devices. (See also unit on Computer Composition.)

The data base of book catalogs and printed indexes is, with the exception of KWIC indexes, created by human catalogers and indexers. The result of the intellectual work of these people is encoded to include information which will allow for the machine manipulation of the content of the individual records. The encoded records are then converted into machine-readable form. Encoding in this case means the recording of the bibliographic information in a form that can subsequently be processed by the computer. This primarily involves the identification of such fields in the record as author, title, publisher, date, etc., so that the computer can recognize these and differentiate between them during processing. This can be achieved by specifying the location and the boundaries of the items through symbols or through their relative position in the record.

Two principal intellectual problems related to the encoding of information are: (1) the determination of which of the elements are potentially useful information access points; and (2) making explicit the content of the data included in the record. The importance of these points was clarified by the study of the problems of recording Library of Congress bibliographic data for machine processing in Project MARC. An example of information that is implicit in a Library of Congress bibliographic entry is the language of the publication. To make it explicit for the computer the name of the language must be spelled out or a numerical code be used, with each language designated by a unique preassigned number. The language of the publication could then be indicated by entering the appropriate number in the record.[1]

Another problem area relates to the duplication of file sequences which have been traditionally used in libraries for manual filing. For example, when the ALA filing rules were examined it was found that, because they are based on so much information that it is implicit rather than explicit in the record, extremely complex programming or extensive data preparation would be required to make the information explicit enough for filing by machine.

Examples of situations where implicit information is used in filing are such things as making a distinction between a personal and a corporate author, filing an abbreviation as if it were spelled out, or filing a type of heading such as U.S.--History--Civil War chronologically rather than alphabetically. In the latter case, to be able to follow ALA rules, the implicit information that the Civil War occurred between 1861 and 1865 needs to be supplied explicitly.

The application of a set of rules, such as those of the ALA, is essentially a two-step process. It involves the application of "conversion rules" and of "sort rules." The two-stage process can be illustrated through the ALA rule which requires that names beginning with M', Mac, and Mc be filed together as if spelled Mac. In human filing the filer must mentally convert such a name as McDonald into MacDonald and then file it alphabetically. When he substitutes MacDonald for McDonald he is applying conversion rules, and when he files it in the order of the alphabet he is applying sort rules. The former requires intellectual effort, the latter is a purely mechanical process. The need for conversion rules of course could be reduced by changing the content and the format of the record so that when filed by machine it could be put into the desired sequence; for example, U.S.--History--1861-1865 (Civil War) if chronological filing is desirable.[2]

The study of filing rules for computerization purposes resulted in the questioning by many of the practical value of such complex rules as the ALA rules, for example. There is reason to believe that many of the filing rules which have been used in libraries are known by the filers only and that users often approach the file without any awareness of its intricate logical arrangement. On this basis there has been a gradual orientation toward simpler filing rules which are easy for both the computer and the user to comprehend.

References

1. Buckland, Lawrence F. The Recording of Library of Congress Bibliographic Data in Machine Form. Washington, D.C., Council on Library Resources, Inc., 1965.
2. Cartright, Kelley L. and Ralph M. Shoffner. Catalogs in Book Form... Institute of Library Research, University of California, 1967.

AUTOMATIC INDEXING

In automatic indexing, index entries are derived by the computer directly from the natural language text of the document. The human effort of creating document descriptions to indicate subject content is eliminated. This type of computer indexing should be carefully distinguished from mechanical storage and retrieval systems in which manually created index records are searched mechanically.

Automatic indexing requires that the text of a document be available in machine-readable form. Since special conversion into machine-readable form is expensive the process becomes more economical when machine-readable transcripts of text can be obtained as a by-product of the reproduction process. While at present such tapes are not always available, as computer composition becomes more widely used more of them should be obtainable, and that should greatly improve the economics of automatic indexing. The general availability of character recognition devices, which are capable of automatically converting print into machine-readable form, will have the same effect.

Intellectually, automatic indexing faces many of the same problems as those encountered in automatic translation. In both cases, progress is difficult because of our inability to produce valid algorithms for the computer for the creation of document descriptions. In both cases we suffer from a lack of understanding of the relationship between meaning and words in text. To index, the computer must derive meaning from strings of characters; and we cannot tell it how to do this since we do not know how we do it ourselves. Sophisticated semantic and linguistic knowledge is lacking, as in the case of automatic translation.

Because of the lack of sophisticated semantic and linguistic knowledge, the automatic indexing methods which have been experimented with have been largely empirical and fairly primitive. They are based on such things as the number of occurrences of words, the co-occurrence of words, the relative position of words, the characteristics of strings of characters constituting words, and comparisons or partial comparisons, with stored dictionaries.

On the basis of data derived through such relatively unsophisticated methods, different researchers have drawn different inferences concerning the usefulness of the various methods for the creation of subject descriptions for documents.

A great deal of research in automatic indexing is the outgrowth of the fundamental work of Hans Peter Luhn, who was the first to use frequency counts as a measure of word significance. This method, while easy to implement by comuter, lacks an underlying theory indicating the significance of high or low frequency of occurrence for the determination of subject content. A number of methods represent variations of refinements of the basic idea of word counting. For example, instead of using the actual text words as index terms on the basis of their frequency, standard subject categories can be assigned based on frequency, or indexing can be based on the co-occurrence of words in text.

Automatic indexing can be based on the comparison of words or parts of words with a stored dictionary, either for the selection of index terms or to prevent certain words from becoming index terms. The latter approach is used in KWIC indexing, the only automatic indexing method in commercial use today.[1,2]

Straight word counting and KWIC indexing both suffer from lack of vocabulary control. Switching from word count to standardized subject terms, or comparisons with stored dictionaries, allows the use of controlled vocabularies and cross-reference systems. However, all methods have the inherent limitation of being dependent on the explicit mention of the subject for it to be indexed.[3] No method has been developed as yet for mechanical indexing of information that is only implicit in the text.

The method generally referred to as automatic abstracting is in fact automatic extracting. In other words, sentences which are judged to be significant are selected from text. Significance is determined through the number of occurrences of high frequency words in the sentence and the linear distance between them caused by the intervention of non-significant words.[4]

The automatic indexing of proper nouns is a problem in itself. While a proper noun is comparatively easy for a human to recognize, it is extremely difficult to define for the purposes of computer processing. If capitalization were used as a basis for selection, in addition to proper nouns, text words capitalized for grammatical reasons and first words of sentences, which are frequently not proper nouns, would also be selected.

Other situations would also have to be taken into consideration by the computer program. In many instances, several proper nouns directly following each other in the text or separated from each other by non-capitalized text words should be picked up as a unit in order to produce a meaningful entry. The most obvious examples of this situation are personal names. It is desirable to have surnames and their accompanying first names and/or initials appear in the index as units, rather than to have the various parts of a name scattered.

Capitalized words constituting a single name may be separated from each other by non-capitalized words, as for example, in some Spanish and German names, or in such corporate names as that of the Library of Congress. These should, of course, be kept together as units. In other cases, proper nouns directly following one another in the text should appear as individual entries in the index. Computer rules would have to be formulated to meet all of these conditions.

Instructions would have to be created to enable the computer to recognize the end of a proper noun unit, even though the words which follow in the text are also proper nouns. For example, in a footnote the computer would have to know where the author's name ends and where the name of the journal begins. Hyphenated names, names in parentheses, etc., are other examples of problems for which provision must be made in the indexing algorithm.

These are only a few examples of the considerations involved in designing a computer program for the indexing of proper nouns which would eliminate the necessity of human post-editing. It is evident that to design such a program it would not only be necessary to identify and define all of the possible situations relating to proper nouns which may arise in natural language, but that computer instructions for handling all of these situations would have to be formulated.[5]

On the whole, while a great deal of interesting experimentation is going on in the area of automatic indexing, additional research is needed, both in linguistics and in the theory of indexing, to develop methods which will compare favorably with good human indexing.

One overall advantage of automatic indexing is its consistency. Whenever the same program is used to process the same text the outcome of the indexing will be the same to a much greater extent than is true in human indexing.

MACHINE TRANSLATION

Research in machine translation--translation of texts from one natural language into another by machine--began as recently as the 1950's and has been supported principally by three major government agencies: the National Science Foundation, the Central Intelligence Agency, and the Department of Defense. By 1965 these agencies had spent a total of $19 million for mechanical translation research, with the DoD leading with $11 million.

The objectives of mechanical translation research have been attractive in view of the increasing need to be aware of information contained in foreign-language materials and the repeated complaints about the scarcity of well qualified human translators. In the last few years, however, the sponsoring agencies have become increasingly skeptical about the possibility of completely automatic translation and have been gradually reducing their support for research in this field.

Representative Machine Applications 181

In 1966 the Automatic Language Processing Advisory Committee of the National Academy of Sciences--National Research Council expressed pessimism about the possibility of achieving machine translation of a quality equal to translation done by human translators, and recommended expenditures in two related areas: (1) computational linguistics--studies in parsing, sentence generation, structure, semantics, and quantitative linguistic matters, including experiments with machine aids or without; (2) improvements of translation--studies which are aimed at increasing the speed and decreasing the cost of translations and which will help to specify degrees of acceptable quality.

The report of the Committee also reflects an interesting change of focus from fully automated machine translation to machine-aided translation, in which the machine is used to help to speed up the human translation process.

The intellectual processes involved in translation from one language into another are somewhat similar to those involved in information retrieval. In the first case we have to translate ideas expressed in one natural language into another, in the second case translation from a natural language to an artificial language is involved.

Machine translation means going by algorithm from machine-readable source text to useful target text without recourse to human translation or editing. The primary reason for failing to develop such an algorithm is our limited understanding of the translation process. When an attempt was made to describe the translation process to the machine, it became evident that we did not have an adequate understanding of the organization and operation of language to enable us to do so. In addition to programming problems related to linguistics, we do not know how to program machines for the extra-linguistic knowledge which the human translator uses to resolve semantic ambiguities. Victor Yngve, an outstanding researcher in the field, summed up the current situation and future prospects of machine translation in the following:

> ...at present it (machine translation) serves no useful purpose without postediting, and with postediting the overall process is slow and uneconomical. As of the possibility of fully automatic translation I am convinced that we will some day reach the point where this will be feasible and economical. However, there is considerable basic knowl-

edge required that we simply don't have at the moment, and it is anybody's guess how soon this knowledge can be obtained.[6]

Experimental Methods of Machine Translation

To produce an acceptable translation the machine is required to do more than just word-for-word translation. The machine has to recognize the sentence structure as well as the message content of every sentence in the text. It must be able to identify correctly to what sentence component each word of text belongs, and in what way these sentence components are related to each other to make up the total structure of the sentence. Because words taken individually very often have a whole range of different meanings, the semantic interpretation of each sentence requires the resolution of complex semantic ambiguities.[7] The experimental methods described here have resolved these problems to a greater or lesser extent.

Item-for-item substitution is the simplest method of processing, in which a word or group of words are converted independently from one language to another. The method is based on extensive stored dictionaries, and text words or phrases are compared with dictionary terms. Whenever a match occurs, the corresponding dictionary term in the target language is substituted. The method is simple in terms of processing but its major limitation is that a given word may have a number of possible equivalents, and we do not have a satisfactory method of programming the machine to pick the right equivalent for a given context.

Morphological processing is more complex, because it takes into account the rules concerning the relationship between derived forms and the basic dictionary forms of words. This method requires the use of a smaller dictionary than item-for-item substitution but it requires a larger and more complex program. Essentially, this method has the same limitations as item-for-item substitution and the quality of the output is about the same for both methods.

Syntactic translation is based on the rules of syntax. This process, to be successful, must take into consideration the syntax of both the source and the target languages. The automatic parsing programs which have been developed have been largely concerned with the analysis of the source language. In syntactic processing some of the problems related to multiple equivalents have been reduced because parsing eliminates those equivalents which are inconsistent with the grammatical categories found through the analysis of the text. However, some multiple equivalents will not be eliminated because several equivalents may be grammatically correct.

Transformational processing is based on the use of transformational grammars both for the analysis of the source language and for the generation of the target language. Transformational grammar includes rules which indicate how various syntactic constructions are related to or may be derived from other constructions which are simpler or more basic. The idea is that it should be possible to establish correspondence between the transformational representations of the source and the target language and that these can be used as a basis for translation.[8]

Machine-Aided Translation

As it became evident that fully automatic high-quality translation is in the somewhat distant future, interest began to shift in the direction of machine-aided translation. The report of the Automatic Language Processing Committee strongly reflects this shift in interest.

In machine-aided translation, the machine is used to produce tools which support and can speed up the human translation process. This concept should be distinguished from "human-aided machine translation," in which human posteditors are used to improve the results of the machine output.

Some machine-aided translation systems use the computer to produce specialized text-related glossaries that are intended to help the human translator. Computer preparation of the text-related dictionary fits into the translation process in the following way. The translator reads the text to be translated and underlines the English words for which he wishes to find the foreign equivalents. Punched cards are prepared for the underlined words. The information on the cards is then fed into the computer, which checks the words against a stored dictionary and prints out the equivalents. In a more sophisticated approach, the entire sentence containing the underlined word is keypunched and put into the computer. The computer then goes through an automatic dictionary look-up routine and prints out the sentence (or sentences) that most closely match (in lexical terms) the sentences in question. In both cases the printouts serve as text-related dictionaries for the human translator.

Tests showed that a translator working with conventional aids requires 66 percent more time, on the average, than a translator working with a text-related dictionary.[6]

References

1. Artandi, Susan. "A Selective Bibliographic Survey of Automatic Indexing Methods," Special Libraries, 54: 632-634, December 1963.

2. Stevens, Mary Elizabeth. Automatic Indexing: A State-of-the-Art Report. Washington, D.C., National Bureau of Standards, 1970. 298p.

3. Artandi, Susan. "Computer Indexing of Medical Articles. Project MEDICO," Journal of Documentation, 25:185-282, September 1969.

4. Edmundson, H. P. "New Methods in Automatic Extracting," Journal of the ACM, 16:264-285, April 1969.

5. Artandi, Susan. "Mechanical Indexing of Proper Nouns," Journal of Documentation, 19:187-196, December 1963.

6. Language and Machines; Computers in Translation and Linguistics. A report by the Automatic Language Processing Advisory Committee, Division of Behavioral Sciences, National Academy of Sciences, National Research Council. Publication 1416. Washington, D.C., National Research Council, 1966.

7. Garvin, Paul L. "Language and Machines," International Science and Technology, pp. 63-76, May 1967.

8. See, Richard. "Mechanical Translation and Related Language Research," Science, 144:621-626, May 8, 1964.

Index

Abstracting, automatic, 179
Address in computer technology, 113
Aiken, Howard, 88
Aitchison, T. M., 167
ALA (American Library Association) filing rules, 176
ALGOL programming language, 121
Alphabetic subject indexing, citation order, 42
American Documentation Institute, Symposium on Education for Information Science, 15-16
See also American Society for Information Science
American Society for Information Science, 19
See also American Documentation Institute
Analog information, 87-88
Annual Review of Information Science and Technology, 16
Artandi, Susan, 23, 34, 60, 61, 81, 82, 184
Assembler, 121
Assembly program, 121
ASTIA (Armed Forces Technical Information Agency), 47
Augmented Catalog Program (of Project Intrex), 169-170
Automatic abstracting, 179
Automatic indexing, 177-180
of proper nouns, 179
Automatic Language Processing Advisory Committee, National Academy of Sciences, National Research Council, 181
Automatic translation
See Mechanical translation
Auxiliary storage, 98, 113, 115-118
Avram, Henriette D., 150

Babbage, Charles, 88
Backward cycling, 57
Batch processing, 123
Batten, William E., 47
Baxendale, Phyllis, 23
Benenfeld, Alan R., 34, 174
Bibliographic coupling, 59
Binary codes, 91
Binary concept, 90-92
Binary mode, 88
Binary notation, 91
Binary number system, 91-92
Bit, 91
Bivona, William A., 166
Boolean operators,
in post-coordinate searching, 50
used to define document sets, 50-51
Borko, Harold, 23
British Classification Research Group, 46
Buckland, Lawrence F., 177

Carbonell, Jaine R., 131
Cartright, Kelley L., 177
Case Western Reserve University Index to Metallurgical Literature, 78-79
relevance study, 79
Cathode-ray tube (CRT) terminals, 127-128
Chaining, 66
Character rate, 99
Chemical Abstracts, 59, 73-74
Chemical Titles, 158
CIM (Computer input microfilm), 104
Citation indexing, 57-60
comparison with subject indexing, 58
Citation order, 41-42
Cleverdon, Cyril W., 34, 60, 61, 75, 79, 82

185

COBOL programming language, 121
Colon Classification, 46
   citation order, 42
COM
   See Computer output microfilm
COMIT programming language, 121-122
Committee on Scientific and Technical Information (COSATI) Guidelines for the Development of Information Retrieval Thesauri, 43
Compiler, 121
Computer composition, 109-110
Computer input microfilm (CIM), 104
Computer output microfilm (COM), 110-111
Computer printout equipment, 106-109
Computer program, 90, 119
Computer typesetting
   See Computer composition
Consistency of indexing, 56-57
Consoles,
   See Terminals
Controlled vocabularies, 36-37, 39-42
Convertability of vocabularies, 37
Cooper, William S., 61
Coordinate indexing, 47-48
   and combination of sets, 50
Coordination, 53
Core storage, 114-115
COSATI
   See Committee on Scientific and Technical Information
Cost-benefit of retrieval systems, 80-81
Cost-effectiveness of retrieval systems, 80
Cranfield evaluation studies, 78-80
Crestadoro, Andrea, 38
CRT displays, 127-128
CRT
   See Cathode ray tube
Cuadra, Carlos A., 16, 23

Data cells, 119

Data retrieval, 26-27
Department of Defense (DoD), manual for Thesaurus preparation, 43
Depth of indexing, 41
Dewey Decimal Classification, 31, 43, 46
Dexter, Margaret E., 61
Dictionaries
   See Thesauri
Digital computer,
   characteristics, 87-90
   organization, 90
   program execution, 90
Dimitry, Donald L., 130
Direct file organization, 48, 65
Disk storage, 116
Document retrieval,
   definition, 26
   evaluation, 74-81
   generalized view, 27-34
   inherent limitations, 28-29
   and set theory, 48-52
   underlying assumptions, 27
DoD
   See Department of Defense
Drum storage, 118

Edmundson, H. P., 184
Education for information science, 20-21
Elkinol, Jerome L., 131
Engineers Joint Council system of roles and links, 55
Enumerative classification schemes, 44
ERIC Rules for Thesaurus Preparation, 43
Evaluation of retrieval systems, 74-81
   evaluative criteria, 75
   measures, 76
   relevance judgments, 77-78
Executive program in time-sharing, 124
Exhaustivity of indexing, 41

Facet analysis, 46
   for thesaurus construction, 43
Faceted classification, 45-46

citation order, 42
Fact retrieval
  See Data retrieval
Fairthorne, Robert A., 22, 28, 34, 68, 81
False coordinations, 48
Feedback, 71-72
File,
  accessing of, 66
  definition of, 63
  processes, 67
  sequences, 66
  structures, 65
File organization,
  direct, 48
  inverted, 47-48
Filing rules for machine sorting, 176-177
Fischer, Margaret, 159
Fixed word length, 112
Format of records, 64
FORTRAN programming language, 121
Forward cycling, 57

Gardin, I. C., 60
Garfield, Eugene, 62
Garvin, Paul L., 184
General purpose computers, 89
Georgia Institute of Technology, 15-16, 21
Gurley, E. J., 34, 174

Harmon, Glynn, 23
Harter, Stephen P., 82
Hierarchical linkage, 54
Hierarchical relationships among index terms, 40
Hines, Theodore C., 60
Housman, Edward M., 166
Huang, Theodore S., 62

Index language devices, 53-55
Index languages, 39-42
  control of, 39-40
  convertability, 37
  effect on retrieval performance, 39
  functions of, 39
  relationships among terms, 40-41

size, 40
specificity, 41
Index Medicus, 59, 135-136
Indexing, automatic, 177-180
Information science
  definitions, 15-17
  education, 20-21
  literature, 19
  relationship with librarianship, 17, 22
Interrecord gap, 99
Intrex (Information Transfer Experiment)
  See Project Intrex
Inverted file organization, 47-48, 65

JOSS (Johnniac Open Shop System), 127

Keen, Michael, 34, 82
Kent, Allen, 23
Kessler, M. M., 174
Key-Word-In-Context,
  See KWIC
Key-Word-Out-of-Context (KWOC) index, 158
KWIC (Key-Word-In-Context) index, 30, 38, 72-73, 151-159
KWOC (Key-Word-Out-of-Context) index, 158

Lancaster, F. W., 60, 61, 82, 83, 145
Landau, Herbert, 167
Lead-in vocabulary, 37-38
Lewis, Robert F., 159
Library of Congress,
  automation program, 145
  MARC record, 64
  MARC system, 145-150
  RECON Project, 146
Licklider, J. C. R., 131
Link, definition, 48, 53
  in post-coordinate systems, 54
Lovins, Julie B., 174
Logical operators
  See Boolean operators

Luhn, Hans Peter, 151, 159, 166, 178

MAC,
  See Project MAC
Machine-aided translation, 183-184
Machine language, 119-120
Machine translation,
  See Mechanical translation
Magnetic core storage, 114-115
Magnetic disk storage, 116
Magnetic drum storage, 118
Magnetic tape, 97-102
  characteristics, 98-99
Main storage, 113-115
Maloney, Ruth Kay, 167
Man/computer interactive systems, 123-130
MARC II record, 64, 107, 146-150
MARC system, 145-150
Maron, M. E., 34, 62
Massachusetts Institute of Technology (MIT),
  Project INTREX, 168-172
  Project MAC, 172-174
Meadow, Charles T., 81, 130
Mechanical translation, 180-184
  experimental methods, 182-183
  machine-aided translation, 183-184
Medical Literature Analysis and Retrieval System (MEDLARS)
  See MEDLARS
MEDLARS (Medical Literature Analysis and Retrieval System), 135-145
  evaluation study, 80, 143-144
  indexing, 136
  input subsystem, 138
  on-line retrieval, 143
  publication subsystem, 140
  retrieval subsystem, 140
  vocabulary, 136
MESH
  See Medical Subject Headings
Medical Subject Headings (MESH) 136
Merging of files, 67
Metcalfe, John, 42, 60

Miller, George A., 23
Mills, Jack, 34, 60, 82
MIT
  See Massachusetts Institute of Technology
Mott, Thomas H., Jr., 130
Multiple data bases, 165-166
Multiprocessing, 125
Multiprogramming, 125

National Electronics Research Council, 165
Nickerson, Raymond S., 131
Number systems, 91-92

Object program, 121
On-line retrieval, 123-124, 168-174
Operating system, 89
Optical character recognition, 103, 104

Paper tape, 95-97
Parity bit, 97
Permuted indexing,
  See KWIC index
PL/1 programming language, 121
Post-coordination, 44, 47-48
  and the combination of sets, 50
Precision devices, 53
Precision ratio, 76
  relationship with recall ratio, 78
Pre-coordinate systems, 44-47
Primary sort key, 64
Printed indexes computer produced, 175-177
Printers
  chain, 107
  print wheel, 107
  wire matrix, 109
Problem-oriented programming languages, 120-123
Processor, 121
Programming languages, 119-123
Project Intrex, 28, 37, 168-172
  Augmented Catalog Program, 169-170
  command language, 171

file organization, 170
stemming algorithm, 170
Text Access Program, 171-172
Project MAC, 172
Technical Information Project, 172-174
Proper noun indexing, 179
Punched card, 95-96

Query formulation, 69-70
QUIKTRAN, 127

Rabinow, Jacob C., 130
RAND Corp. JOSS (Johnniac Open Shop System), 127
RAND Tablet, 105
Random access, 66
Ranganathan, S.R., 42, 46, 60
Read property, 113
Read/write time, 99
Recall devices, 53-54
Recall ratio, 76
relationship with precision ratio, 78
RECON (Retrospective Conversion Project), 146
Records, structure of, 64
Rees, Alan M., 79, 82
Register, in computer technology, 112-113
Reimers, Paul R., 150
Relevance judgments in document retrieval, 77-78
Relevance ratio
See Precision ratio
Roles, definition, 48, 53
in post-coordinate systems, 54-55
Rust, J.E., 34, 174

SABRE American Airlines reservation system, 127
Sarocevic, Tefko, 82
Science Citation Index, 59
SDI
See Selective Dissemination of Information
Searching, 67-74
effect of vocabulary control, 72-74
formulation of search strategy, 68, 71-72
query formulation, 69-70
role of feedback, 71
Secondary sort key, 65
See, Richard, 184
Selective Dissemination of Information (SDI), 160-167
cost, 165
description, 160-161
evaluation, 165
feedback, 162
matching strategies, 163-165
user profiles, 161-163
Sequential access, 66
Sequential order, 66
Sets,
definition of, 48
membership in, 48-49
combination of, 50-51
subsets, 49-50
and document retrieval, 48-52
Shannon, Claude, 89, 130
Shaw, Ralph R., 21, 23
Shoffner, Ralph M., 34, 62, 177
SNOBOL programming language, 121-122
Sort key, 64
Sorting, 67
Source program, 121
Special purpose computer, 89
Specificity of index terms, 41
Spencer, C.C., 62
SPIRES, 124
St. Laurent, C.M., 61
State University of New York Biomedical Communications Network, 124
Stemming algorithms, 170
Stender, Robert C., 130
Stevens, Mary Elizabeth, 184
Stiller, Joy D., 145
Stoplist, 152
Storage, 112-119
auxiliary, 98, 113, 115-118
magnetic core, 114-115
magnetic disk, 115
magnetic drum, 118
main, 114-115
random access, 114-115
Struminger, Leny, 130
Subject authority list,
See Thesauri

Subject indexing, 35-37
   vocabulary control, 36-37, 39-42
Subordinate sort key, 64-65
Subsets, 49-50
Supervisory program in time-sharing, 124
Swanson, Don, 61, 79, 82
Symbolic programming languages, 120
Synthetic classification schemes, 44, 46
System vocabulary, 37-38

Taube, Mortimer, 47, 54, 61, 79, 82
Terminals, 127-128
   Cathode ray tube (CRT), 127-128
   teletype, 127
Text Access Program (of Project Intrex), 171-172
TEXT-PAC, 70
Thesauri, 42-43
   use as a searching aid, 43
Time-sharing systems, 123-130
   dedicated data base, 127
   definition, 124
   general purpose, 125
   human factors in, 129-130
   memory protection, 125
   special purpose, 127
   types, 125-126
Translation, automatic, 180-184
Translation, computer-aided 183-184

Uniterms, 47
Universal Decimal Classification, 44, 46
   citation order, 41

Variable word length, 112
Venn diagrams, 52
Vickery, B. C., 60
Vocabulary control, 39
Voice output, 111-112
Voice recognition, 104-105

WADEX (Word and Author Index), 158
Wall, Eugene, 167
Walter, Gerard O., 130
Warheit, I. A., 81
Weighting, 53
   in SDI Systems, 164
Weitzman, Coy, 130
Western Reserve University
   See Case Western Reserve University
Word-and-Author-Index (WADEX), 158
Word, in computer technology, 112
Word indexing, 37-39
   from titles, 38
   limitations, 38-39
Write property, 113

Yerkes, Charles P., 130
Yngve, Victor, 181

Zunde, Pranas, 61